Foreword by

GEORGE GUZZARDO

PARADIGM SHIFT

7 REALITIES OF SUCCESS IN THE NEW ECONOMY

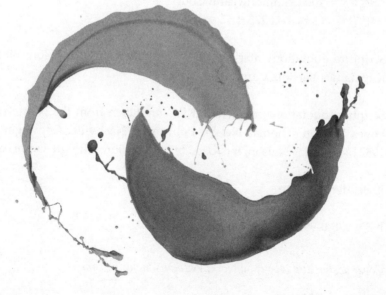

Life Leadership Essentials Series

First Edition, December 2015
10 9 8 7 6 5 4 3 2 1

Published by:

Obstaclés Press
200 Commonwealth Court
Cary, NC 27511

Scripture quotations marked "KJV" are taken from the Holy Bible, King James Version, Cambridge, 1769.

Scripture quotations marked "NKJV" are taken from the New King James Version, Thomas Nelson Publishers, Nashville. Copyright © 1982 by Thomas Nelson, Inc. Used by permission. All rights reserved.

lifeleadership.com

ISBN 978-0-9970293-3-8

Cover design and layout by Norm Williams, nwa-inc.com

Printed in the United States of America

Twenty years from now,
what will you wish you had done today?
— CHRIS BRADY

CONTENTS

FOREWORD

Does anyone believe that the same industrial society business and educational principles that applied in the nineteen hundreds would apply in the Information Age? Yet that's exactly what many are still trying to do. *Paradigm Shift: 7 Realities of Success in the New Economy* provokes thought about why we do things the way we do, and it opens up new insights about what leaders could accomplish in the new economy if they were to see things a little differently. It changes perceptions about the future because it presents solutions that break currently perceived limitations. As the text says, "Leaders foresee and influence the big shifts and, most important, coming realities."

This book has the potential to stimulate some thought-provoking discussions. It goes into depth about our current paradigms, such as the education paradigm in which students are graded largely based on their ability to memorize and agree with the views of accepted experts. In this paradigm, colleges are designed to enroll students, garner research funds, and accrue status through rankings and scholarly articles but not to make sure students graduate prepared to thrive in the modern economy. In addition to confronting such current accepted behaviors, this book offers common-sense solutions to some of the challenges we are facing today in the areas of leadership, education, health care, media, personal life, and business.

The question is posed: "When is the best time to plant a shade tree?" Answer: twenty years ago. Leaders have the opportunity to act today so those living twenty years from now will benefit. *Paradigm Shift* is a leadership mandate that if taken seriously can change reality for future generations, bringing shared benefits to communities all over and helping people to prosper and thrive in the modern economy embracing the new ways of doing things.

Don't just read through this book. Think through this book, and be prepared to act on what you learn.

—George Guzzardo
September 2015, Arizona

PROLOGUE

The story is frequently told of a man in China many years ago who was asked by a friend how his family was doing. "Pretty well," he responded, "except that my son was recently injured in a farm accident."

"That's terrible!" replied his friend.

"Not really," the man said. "Just a few days later, the military came and impressed all the young men his age into their service and took them away to the wars, but my son was spared."

"Ohhhh," his friend replied.

That's a paradigm shift.

An accident and injury sounded bad. But it turned out to be a blessing.

A paradigm ('perə,dīm) shift is a sudden, major change in the way you view something, brought on by new information or a new detail that was formerly unknown.

> A paradigm shift is a sudden, major change in the way you view something, brought on by new information or a new detail that was formerly unknown.

Stephen Covey spoke of riding the subway one evening after a busy day and being frustrated as another man let his rowdy children make noise, bother other passengers, and generally misbehave. He finally asked the man if he would please take better care of his children.

The man apologized and then said that he had just come from the hospital where his wife, the children's mother, had died an hour earlier and that he was letting them behave as they chose, happy that they weren't totally depressed.

Wow! Paradigm shift.

Imagine how Stephen must have felt, looking on in horror and wishing he had kept quiet, as the man pulled his children together and told them to behave.[1]

> A true paradigm shift can shake us right down to the toes.

Paradigm shifts are often incredibly powerful. They don't just change our minds; they can deeply impact our feelings as well. A true paradigm shift can shake us right down to the toes.

Covey wrote: "The term *paradigm shift* was introduced by Thomas Kuhn in his highly influential landmark book, *The Structure of Scientific Revolutions*. Kuhn shows how almost every significant breakthrough in the field of scientific endeavor is first a break with tradition, with old ways of thinking, with old paradigms."[2]

Paradigm shifts occur in personal life, family, education, work, art, business, and every other walk of life. They dramatically influence everyone they touch, leaving a legacy of major change in their path.

This book is about seven such paradigm shifts, seven major emerging changes that will rock the world in the years and decades just ahead.

In fact, in the famous words of Patrick Henry on the eve of another world-changing paradigm shift:

> *They have already begun....*

In short, if you don't already know about these seven shifts

Paradigm shifts occur in personal life, family, education, work, art, business, and every other walk of life.

and use them in your daily leadership, you're already behind the curve. Leaders need to deeply understand these seven paradigm shifts that are remaking the world in their image.

INTRODUCTION

For if the trumpet makes an uncertain sound, who will prepare for battle?
—1 CORINTHIANS 14:8, NKJV

Perception is reality…except when it isn't.

And truth be told, it *usually* isn't! In fact, if we're really going to be accurate about this, *reality* is reality.

Perception sometimes falls short. But big problems arise when our perceptions about the world tell us one thing, and the reality is something different.

Sometimes things aren't as they seem. As the nineteenth-century French writer Frédéric Bastiat taught, some things are seen, while other things are not seen. And it is those things that are not seen that can really surprise us and cause major challenges—unless we pay attention to them early on.

This book is about seven new realities in our world and how understanding them can help prepare us to become *real* leaders. The way we perceive these realities will have a huge impact on how we face them and the success and leadership we choose in the years ahead.

Arthur Schopenhauer said, "Every man takes the limits of his own field of vision for the limits of the world." Not only is the tendency to confuse perception for reality a common trend among moderns; it has been an important human struggle for a very long time.

Not a Democracy

But, as bestselling author Orrin Woodward puts it, "Truth is not a democracy." Despite the fact that people frequently seem to mistake perception for reality and always have, doing so is *still* just that—a mistake!

> Despite the fact that people frequently seem to mistake perception for reality and always have, doing so is *still* just that—a mistake!

The key is to make your perceptions reflect the truth, the actual reality. In other words, make sure the map matches the territory.

Stephen Covey called this "paradigm," Woodward called it the "Lens Effect," and others have called it many things—from plain old "perception" to "worldview" to Einstein's "relative position in time and space."

> Whatever label you prefer, your paradigm makes a huge difference in the way you interact with—and in—the real world.

Whatever label you prefer, your paradigm makes a huge difference in the way you interact with—and in—the real world. This is central to leadership. Getting it right is essential.

Steve Maraboli added to this concept when he said, "Your agreement with reality defines your life." Note that he says it will define your life, but he very clearly does *not* say it will change reality itself. No matter how long a person sits around believing purple is orange, it will remain what it really is, unless it undergoes real and actual change.

The Wizard of Oz by L. Frank Baum taught some interesting lessons on the topic of paradigm and perception. For example, what color is the Emerald City?

Most people who have seen the movie but haven't read the book will answer, "Green—it's obvious! In fact, that's why it's called 'emerald.'"

> **No matter how long a person sits around believing purple is orange, it will remain what it really is, unless it undergoes real and actual change.**

Interestingly enough, it's actually a white city, in which inhabitants and visitors are forced to wear goggles with green lenses. This gives the whole place the appearance of being green. Because it seems green, everyone acts accordingly, and the things they "know" about the real world are consequently somewhat limited.

Likewise, those who have only experienced the movie representation of the city assume it really is green and therefore miss the whole lesson on paradigm: If it's just a green city, what does it have to teach about green-tinted goggles?

The point is this: perception is not always reality, but it is certainly important because it influences the real actions of individuals, businesses, organizations, nations, etc.

The Past Is in the Past

Moreover, one of the biggest determinants of our perceptions is the way things *have* been for the last twenty-five years. If you are younger than twenty-five, then of course this is true. Obviously your time alive dominates your perception. After all, what else is there? But if you became an adult any time in the last twenty-five years, meaning that you're still younger than forty-five, you've spent your entire adult life living with the perception that reality is what you've just experienced.

And even if you're older than forty-five, you're a lot more likely to think the next twenty-five years will be like the last twenty-five than you are to believe that the future will be like things were when you were a kid or that they'll be some totally new reality that hasn't quite presented itself yet.

But things do change. A key reality is that some realities are changing—right now. Just as the Internet has drastically changed a number of things about society in the past decades, other changes are occurring even as you read this book.

In short, it is absolutely certain that—given the way things work, especially in this age of rapid technological advancement—some very important aspects of the next twenty-five years will be drastically different.

Those who operate on the basis that little is going to change, simply acting as if everything will stay the same, will (in most cases) have plenty of time to figure out the new realities after they come along. Indeed, this is exactly what most people do. But the sad truth is that this is also one of the reasons most people aren't leaders.

The Difference That Makes *All* the Difference

Leaders do it differently. You can't lead if you're behind the curve. You can't lead by waiting for massive changes to come, slowly adjusting, and then suddenly one day guiding those you lead innovatively or dynamically. In such cases, by the time your perception gets around to accepting important changes, the people you thought you were leading are already following someone else.

As John Maxwell reminds us, if you're leading and no one is following, you're just out for a walk.

> You can't lead if you're behind the curve.

> By the time your perception gets around to accepting important changes, the people you thought you were leading are already following someone else.

Leaders keep a close eye on the horizon. They don't necessarily know every little change or specific detail that is coming, but they pay attention to what is needed in their family, community, business, industry, and the economy and society as a whole.

By keeping track of changing needs, they have a strong sense of what it will take for society to address those needs. This helps them clearly differentiate between the realities in society and what are mere perceptions.

It also empowers leaders to go beyond preparing for coming changes and to actually *influence* those changes. This is an essential skill of leadership: understanding coming changes well enough to take action now, action that provides the right kind of solutions in the years and decades just ahead. In fact, because of this, real leaders actually *shape* reality.

Shade at High Noon

Bestselling author Chris Brady taught this important principle by asking the old proverbial question, "When is the best time to plant a shade tree?" The answer, of course, is twenty years ago, thus making the tree big enough *today* to provide actual shade. This concept illustrates the leadership ability to deal with reality even when popular perceptions assume something different.

While it may seem difficult and pointless to be planting the tree at such a time—long before you even need shade—waiting until it is desperately needed is the same as waiting until it's too late to make a real and meaningful difference. That's the opposite of leadership.

Some might scoff at the man who spends hours of work and energy planting and cultivating a tree that won't give him any benefit for decades to come, yet there's no better time to put in the work.

Indeed, those who wait until changes and needs are obvious can sometimes survive and even thrive when challenges arise. However, only those who anticipate and act long before the climax of change are true leaders and innovators.

> **Leaders foresee and influence the big shifts and most important emerging realities.**

In short, leaders must take charge of their perceptions and understand the true realities and coming changes. Leaders foresee and influence the big shifts and most important emerging realities.

The Super Seven

The seven paradigm shifts outlined in this book are just such realities. While most people in the masses tend to have a different perception about how these seven trends might unfold (or may not think about them at all), leaders need to be busy, right now, understanding these developments, considering the ramifications, and taking effective action.

Twenty-five years from now, shifts in these seven areas will be obvious. Now is the time for leaders to lead.

Knowing how these seven new realities are restructuring our society, nation, economy, and families is vital information for the innovators, entrepreneurs, and other leaders who will shape the world for the next generation.

What are these seven huge changes that are creating a paradigm shift for our whole society in the years ahead? Leaders want to know....

PARADIGM
1

Networking Is the New Media

The vertical to horizontal power shift that networks bring about will be enormously liberating for individuals. Hierarchies promote moving up and getting ahead, producing stress, tension, and anxiety. Networking empowers the individual, and people in networks tend to nurture one another.

—JOHN NAISBITT

Not shockingly, shifts in reality often come with advances in technology. Sometimes, when technology really "brings it" at the highest level, society undergoes significant changes to keep up.

This is evident in the study of media through the history of the world, and understanding where we've been—tracking and considering past shifts and the early clues that made them obvious to top leaders before they hit full swing—can help

> Sometimes, when technology really "brings it" at the highest level, society undergoes significant changes to keep up.

prospective leaders today see and recognize the signs apparent in our own shifting world.

Interactive Media

For our pioneer ancestors, in the era before mass media, obtaining information about news and current events looked a bit different than it does for us today. For instance, rather than depending on news channels, newspapers or periodicals, and websites, people relied on personal letters, speeches from local leaders and thinkers, and sermons from respected individuals.

They also treasured and repeatedly read a few key books, such as the Bible, the works of Shakespeare, and Plutarch's classic book *Parallel Lives.*

Before 1950, the principal way to obtain news, current events, and media for *most people* was to turn the page and read. Whether in books, the local newspaper, pamphlets, magazines, or somewhere else, the variety of resources for learning and discovering what was going on in the world and what mattered was basically limited to the combination of paper and ink, concerts and plays, and lectures and sermons.

Through such hard-copy or in-person venues, people were able to learn of topics, concepts, facts, world and historical events, and the prominent opinions and arguments about them and also to enjoy music and entertainment.

Journalists, philosophers, musicians, and artists spent their days investigating and determining their message to the public and then getting it to printers or scribes who spent their days making it available to the masses. People loved their weekly church meeting or trips to the general store at least in part because these were sources of news.

Political debates were high drama—the "reality television" of the era. People frequently traveled many miles and even days to attend, like they did with the famous Lincoln–Douglas debates.

In this system, authority and acclaim didn't necessarily come from credentials or expertise. Instead, people listened to those they trusted and respected, those who spoke truths that resonated with them, and the people who just plain made sense.

This system certainly had its benefits, bringing depth, requiring action, and forcing readers and audiences to more fully dig into and ultimately *understand* what they were experiencing. Media was naturally interactive.

As bestselling author Oliver DeMille said:

Books are better than television, the Internet, or the computer for educating and maintaining freedom. Books matter because they state ideas and then attempt to thoroughly prove them. They have an advantage *precisely because they slow down the process,* allowing the reader to internalize, respond, react and transform.

The ideas in books matter because time is taken to establish truth, and because the reader must take time to consider each idea and either accept it or, if he rejects it, to think through sound reasons for doing so. A nation of people who write and read is a nation with the attention span to earn an education and a free society if they choose.

As this quotation subtly implies, a people who reads and thinks is not the only important aspect of a free and educated society. The people must also *write*.

> A people who reads and thinks is not the only important aspect of a free and educated society. The people must also *write*.

Before Snail Mail

In the old information system, letters played a pivotal role in the education and media-sharing segment of society. In the old American West, for example, letters would often be addressed from families on the East Coast in the following fashion:

Jethro Stark
Wyoming or Montana

Such letters would be carried to towns in these or even neighboring territories or states, and sometimes they'd sit at a certain general store, which doubled as the post office in most towns, until a passing cowboy or other traveler would say he was headed to Wyoming, and the store owner would ask him to take the letter with him.

Travelers knew to give their name to the general store owner, who kept a mental tally of whose letters were collecting dust on the store shelf. Amazingly, many of these letters eventually found their way to the addressees.

We can see in examples like the correspondence of John and Abigail Adams, the Jefferson–Madison letters, and the famous fictional and real-life letters by Jane Austen, among others, that writing letters was not only the accepted way to share family news or the latest local developments. It was also an important way to discuss and share powerful ideas and current events and also to learn meaningful things.

Letters were the leading media of the era. And note that this medium replaced the even older model of the traveling minstrel.

> **Writing letters was not only the accepted way to share family news or the latest local developments. It was also an important way to discuss and share powerful ideas and current events and also to learn meaningful things.**

By participating in the media, not only through reading but also through writing about and discussing thoughts, principles, concepts, and events in letters and correspondence, people of these times gained powerful depth and wisdom and were better prepared to understand other media that came their way. This helped them judge the value and truth of the lectures, sermons, books, pamphlets, and other ideas they encountered in the wider media.

For example, when the *Federalist Papers* came out, published as New York newspaper commentaries, the regular citizens were able to closely read and analyze them, even though today these are considered some of the most detailed and intricate political writings of all time.

As the people scrutinized and discussed such concepts and built *relationships* of thinking and evaluating media through letters and other interactions, they were better able to recognize bad political policies, destructive ideas, and negative media in general.

This was a powerful era for media, and the level of general education and enlightenment in the people was among the highest in history. When Tocqueville visited America, he considered this quality of communication a significant contributor to American freedoms.

Of course, local newspapers, pamphlets, books, and even letters also have their limits. While they mostly managed to make it work, the Old West postal system shows that this method of media distribution tended to be somewhat unreliable, time-consuming, and difficult. It was often very slow.

As a result, over time, technology shifted, and with it, reality.

Passive Media

In the 1920s, radio became a major player in the media game, and it continued to boom for the next few decades.

Now it is part of almost every North American home.[3] The irony of this development is, of course, that a smaller percentage of people actually use it in their residences.

This advancement in technology naturally brought a shift to the way people got their news, ideas, opinions, music, etc. Turning on the radio is easier than walking to the porch to fetch the paper, driving to the store to pick up a book, or even settling your record on the record player. Listening to a broadcast is *much* easier than reading through the paper or a book or waiting in line and sitting through an entire concert or lecture.

And picking up the phone is much simpler than pulling out paper and pen, composing a letter, writing it all down, and finding the next cowboy to carry it to Arizona.

Of course, you know the rest. Before long came television, and that practically sealed the deal. As TV became the primary media source, media became less active, less participative, and at the same time more authoritative, credentialist-oriented, and top-down.

In the words of a popular song of the era, "Video killed the radio star."

This brought a significant change, though few people realized it. Over time, as the "experts" on television gained increased credibility in the eyes of the public, many people started losing trust in their own

> Over time, as the "experts" on television gained increased credibility in the eyes of the public, many people started losing trust in their own ideas.

ideas, the wisdom of those who spoke the most truth, or even the people who made the most sense. Instead, they listened to those who had the right title or position, spoke from the right podium, or held the fanciest degree, office, or media platform.

Soon experts ruled the day.

In this era of passive media, people moved away from letters and started using phones for trivial or routine conversation. They increasingly got their news, ideas, and information from trained "experts" and professionals.

Letters, lectures, and sermons were replaced by accredited colleges, classes, and professors, along with TV specials and broadcasts. Instead of sitting around discussing the modern equivalents of the *Federalist Papers*, families would gather around the TV and "learn the facts from those who know what they're talking about."

> **Instead of sitting around discussing the modern equivalents of the *Federalist Papers*, families would gather around the TV.**

Entertainment came straight to our living rooms from Hollywood, New York, or Washington professionals with training at prestigious schools. Information and understanding came from those "licensed" to have an opinion and the textbooks, newspapers, and interviews they approved.

Schools shifted from reading and discussing the great classics, biographies, and ideas from history to studying what the "qualified" elites had to say about them. Youth were graded as "good" or "failing" students largely based on how well they could memorize and agree with the views of the accepted experts.

During World War II, communities looked forward all week to the matinées at the theater, where they'd go to see the weekly movie, and before the movie, everyone sat and watched the government-provided newsreels. In some ways, this was even worse propaganda than reliance on regular professionals and experts because many people went beyond giving too much weight to elites and joined the realm of dependence on government for their news and many of their views on the issues.

The Era of Dependence

Such reliance epitomized the era of passive media. While it made information, news, and current events readily available to the masses, this widespread dependence on the expert–government nexus came with some clear dangers and significant limits.

Winston Churchill said, "Nothing would be more fatal than for the government of states to get in the hands of experts. Expert knowledge is limited knowledge, and the unlimited ignorance of the plain man who knows where it hurts is a safer guide than any rigorous direction of a specialized character."

This is a powerful concept when applied to government, but it also has important application in all aspects of society and especially for the flow of knowledge, ideas, information, and the media. As mentioned, those who control the news also largely control society's views.

While experts can very effectively get their message to their audience in the passive mass media system, and an audience that believes whatever the experts say is often good at carrying out the beliefs and ideas of such experts, this system clearly does not strengthen independent thinking, freedom, and truth.

Earlier, we quoted Orrin Woodward saying that truth isn't a democracy, and we'll add that it shouldn't be an oligarchy dominated by a few licensed or popular professionals either.

In fact, when the people put complete trust in a professional class of media, you have at best a poor guardian of truth and wisdom. And more often, you get an actual enemy to one or the other or to both.

> **When the Establishment in a society controls the ideas and more specifically the popular perception of "the truth," freedom and prosperity are in real danger.**

When the Establishment in a society controls the ideas and more specifically the popular perception of "the *truth*," freedom and prosperity are in real danger. Selfish power seekers throughout history have openly declared that control of the ideas flowing through society is a vital step in obtaining control of society itself.

Consider the words of Joseph Stalin when he said, "We would not let our enemies have guns; why should we let them have ideas?" Mao famously said that "power grows out of the barrel of a gun," but what he proved with Chinese communism and what has been shown in various other historical regimes is that every bit as powerful, if not *more* powerful, than bullets is what comes out of the mouth of a government-paid expert—addressed to listeners conditioned to simply believe.

On the flip side, James Madison said that "the advancement and diffusion of knowledge is the only guardian of true liberty." In the free nations of the twentieth century, government didn't control media in a dictatorial fashion, and the free press allowed wider views to be shared. But still, the widespread reliance on expertise and credentialism had a limiting effect.

> "The advancement and diffusion of knowledge is the only guardian of true liberty."
> —James Madison

Another Change

The proliferation of private cable news operations in the latter quarter of the twentieth century allowed diverse views to be considered once again by larger numbers of citizens, leaving the people the responsibility to sort through information and draw their own conclusions on the issues.

Soon thereafter, with the growth of the Internet worldwide, more people began to doubt the omniscience and omnipotence of the Establishment—and of "the truth" as portrayed by mass media. As the expert monopoly of truth weakens because of how easily anyone can share their thoughts in the Internet era, an interesting development is taking place.

Put simply—and fortunately for the future of freedom and prosperity—advancement in technology is catalyzing an important shift in modern media. The official "experts" are losing power because fewer people now implicitly believe them.

> The people, the masses, are growing less impressed by big media and other traditional institutions and losing trust in them.

Their influence is still strongly felt in many large institutions—both public and private—but the people, the masses, are growing less impressed by big media and other traditional institutions and losing trust in them.

This is where a massive paradigm shift is occurring in the world's communications.

Interactive Media 2.0

Alvin Toffler predicted this shift when he wrote in his book *Powershift* about what he called "gods in white coats." This refers to the massive power wielded by medical doctors in the decades before the Information Age.

For example, from the 1940s through the 1970s, when a doctor told a patient a diagnosis and a treatment, the words of the medical professional were frequently received almost at the level of Scripture. Few people in this era even *considered* arguing with, discounting, or rejecting a doctor's decree.

Today, and ever since the advent of the Internet, the normal response to a doctor's words is to research both his or her diagnosis and treatment plan online, seeking all kinds of alternatives, information, and differing treatment options, both medical and otherwise.

If what the patient reads online differs even slightly from the doctor's expert recommendations, most people today are quick to seek a second or even third opinion. Indeed, today's patients are just as likely to read blogs from half a dozen other patients with the same diagnosis and pay closer attention and apply what they read more rigorously than anything the doctor prescribes.

Doctors are no longer "gods in white coats." People listen to the doctor, but only as one voice among many. And amazingly, many of them turn to their community of patients with their most important questions and needs.

> **Doctors are no longer "gods in white coats."**

We will address this phenomenon further in the chapter entitled "Wellness Is the New Health Care," but we share it here because it is indicative of a broad trend that is influencing nearly every facet of society. We now get our information from a wide range of sources, and frankly, an increasing number of people give more credence to the personal thoughts and experiences of other regular people than to the claims of those boasting expertise or titles.

Experts are out of vogue almost everywhere except in big institutions, and big institutions are falling out of fashion as well. They are being replaced by networks.

> **Experts are out of vogue almost everywhere except in big institutions, and big institutions are falling out of fashion as well.**

In fact, *networks are the new media*. This is the crux of Interactive Media 2.0.

The Rise of the Network

People are now more likely to get their news and current events online, and they tend to trust ordinary people who feel like their peers rather than blindly trusting the experts or professionals. TV remains a source of media products and news today, but its power and monopoly are decreasing as personal and group networks—often using the Internet—get bigger and bigger.

In fact, even though many people still watch TV to keep an eye on current events, most of them approach it differently than they did in past decades. For example, most people *don't* watch news from both sides of an issue.

Instead, they pick the news programs and channels that fit with their network—the people they've tended to agree with, the ones they trust to say the things they think are true. Only a very small percentage of the population routinely watches *both* Fox News and MSNBC.

In past eras, people watched whatever was on and "learned" what the experts taught. Now people tend to watch what they believe, what they agree with, and what they *like*.

If nothing "good" is on TV, they turn to their DVR, or they simply search YouTube, Netflix, Hulu, or some other source to find something they actually care about rather than being held hostage by experts or TV programmers.

As time passes, people are getting more of their news from online sources they trust and listening to the opinions of people in their networked community.

On top of this, most people tend to base their *opinions* of what they watch on things they read on their favorite blogs, conversations they have with friends on Facebook, or YouTube or TED talks on the topic that simply make the most sense.

Increasingly, people give more weight to the words of those they've tended to agree with in the past — not because of any credential, title, or position but because they *seem* right.

Instead of television, people are giving more and more weight to online forums, blogs, training videos, and important conversations, texts, and e-mails. In fact,

> Mirroring the letters, sermons, and debates of the past eras of interactive media centuries ago, the new reality of networking is reemphasizing bottom-up control of ideas and increased control over the media in the hands of the people.

by the time you read this, the names of the latest online and social media providers will likely be in flux. They are always in flux, nowadays more than ever.

Mirroring the letters, sermons, and debates of the past eras of interactive media centuries ago, the new reality of networking is reemphasizing bottom-up control of ideas and increased control over the media in the hands of the people. This is empowering.

And it is causing people to write again, in every e-mail, tweet, post, blog, etc. This requires deeper thinking, even on shallow topics.

The people run the conversation and drive communication according to their own ideas. The media are no longer run by a few managers at the top. (The companies that still *are* run this way are losing market share.)

> **The media are no longer run by a few managers at the top.**

Some of the new networks replacing old-style media consist of Twitter followers, Facebook friends, YouTube stars, community peers online, and a bunch of random strangers who just make sense. These are people you "connect with," "friend," listen to, watch, e-mail, text, tweet, read, blog to, etc.

This is your network.

And the people who influence you most can change today. And then again next week. Easily. It's up to you.

Networks Can Increase Leadership

In a way, this is extremely powerful because it gets the regular people more actively thinking and choosing what to believe. Rather than assuming one person has all the answers because he or she has a badge that says so, people are left to hear both sides and weigh the differing stances before they really form an opinion.

Of course, there is a danger here as well, since people tend to choose a side first and then rarely listen to what anyone else has to say on the subject, reserving the right to post offensive or slanderous memes on other people's Facebook pages.

Sometimes people in the Networking Age of media get too focused on the things they already know, think, or believe, but there is also real potential for important trust, respect, merit, and genuine mentoring.

When people listen to voices they think are right because they make sense, there's more room for positive community and leadership than when they think they *have* to follow simply because someone has the right uniform or works for the right media company.

It is increasingly true that people look to their personal online and other networks for news, friendship, entertainment, communication, opinions, and even values — whatever their "network" is. This network often includes coworkers, but only the people you *talk* to during your work hours. It *doesn't* include the ones you don't talk to or don't want to learn from.

Naturally, anyone who sends you anything on your smartphone has a place in your network—smartphones *themselves* play a vital role in the network. In the Networking Age, when people search online, they search for sources that agree with them, unless their phone is specifically assigned to do otherwise.

Leaders Pay Attention

This trend is set to continue and grow, and we are already seeing a huge shift from Establishment control of society's conversations and ideas to more independence and power in the people.

Leaders who want to make an important contribution in the new reality must understand this powerful paradigm shift.

This gives important influence and power to those who hope to share a message on a broad scale because they no longer have to spend years and decades obtaining the proper titles and positions to be heard by the masses. In fact, in many cases, their time would be better spent honing their message and building a following online or in their networks.

This is not always the case because the shift is still just beginning, but knowing where it's headed—and understanding that the direction of the shift is from mass media to personal community networks—will drastically change the way leaders behave in the economy and world ahead.

As more real leaders learn and understand the changing tide of media in the world and exert their power to meaningfully influence the conversation and put their minds to deeply studying and understanding current events and great ideas, this shift to Interactive Media 2.0 has the potential to bring greater enlightenment, education, understanding, and wisdom to society.

Of course you have to ignore the various trolls, haters, and other distractions that try to infiltrate your network, but most people quickly learn to do this when they start using the Internet, and such voices are much easier to discount than the Establishment experts of the last era.

> **This shift to Interactive Media 2.0 has the potential to bring greater enlightenment, education, understanding, and wisdom to society.**

Most people have learned that there is usually an agenda behind negativity online and the bashing that goes on. Some of it, to be sure, is just "jerks being jerks," but much of it is actually intentional digital assassination sponsored by one entity against another. People have rightly learned to discount such insincerity for the propaganda that it is.

> **More people have the chance to be leaders than ever before in the history of the world.**

To summarize this exciting trend: More people have the chance to be leaders than ever before in the history of the world. Some will use this opportunity. Others will not. Leaders will grasp this shift and act on it—early and often.

Those who do this will experience higher levels of leadership on the wave of this shift, earning increased freedom and prosperity and greater levels of personal success and happiness as well as influence.

Media Senses

Note that in all this, the various types of media appeal to different important human senses. Written media appeal to the mind, to thinking, pondering, considering, analyzing, etc. Auditory media appeal primarily to emotions, to feelings. And the visual media of television and the Internet appeal to the passions, dreams, goals, and visions people have for themselves, those around them, and their immediate life.

This is another way in which the medium of networking is creating powerful opportunities for increased leadership and progress because the networking media format naturally appeals to, stimulates, teaches, and informs a person's interactive and interpersonal senses. Networking is about better relationships, partnerships, and team successes.

> **Networking is about better relationships, partnerships, and team successes.**

Multidimensional Media

The medium of networks naturally emphasizes group goals and cooperative projects. In this way, it is multidimensional media, not focused on one sense or level such as written, auditory, or visual media. Of course, multimedia approaches that combined audiovisual or written-auditory programs were already a Second Level source of media. Networks take us to a Third Level, where all the others are present but relationships and team dynamics are the main currency.

Networks of networks are a Fourth Level, and because of the relationship-oriented nature of networks, they form the building blocks of many more potential levels of success. While most of Information Age society is now moving from the written into a full-fledged visual culture — based around screens and the images and sounds they project — those who are immersed in networks are ahead of the game.

Once the transition to a visual culture is complete, the next step will be the emergence of a network culture. Those who are already learning to network and build networks that flourish in an environment

> Those who are already learning to network and build networks that flourish in an environment of networks are driving the curve.

of networks are driving the curve. They'll be the leaders and innovators. They already are.

Crumbling Pyramids

The great breakthroughs of the twenty-first century will happen in networks.[4] Bestselling author John Naisbitt wrote:

> For centuries, the pyramid structure was the way we organized and managed ourselves. From the Roman Army to the Catholic Church to the organization charts of General Motors and IBM, power and communication have flowed in an orderly manner from the pyramid's top, down to its base; from the high priest, the general, the CEO perched at the very tip, down through the wider ranks of lieutenants and department managers clustered in the middle to the workers, foot soldiers, and true believers at the bottom.
>
> The pyramid structure has been praised and blamed, but its detractors have never come up with a better or more successful framework for organizations...[5]

Until now, that is.

Naisbitt goes on to praise the concept of networks and network leadership in profound terms:

> The failure of hierarchies to solve society's problems forced people to talk to one another — and that was the beginning of networks. In a sense, we clustered together among the ruins of the tumbled-down

pyramid to discuss what to do....That was the birth of the networking structure....

Now the new networking model we have all used with extraordinary success is replacing the hierarchical form we have grown to associate with frustration, impersonality, inertia, and failure....In the network environment, rewards come by empowering others, not by climbing over them.[6]

If you are a leader today, ask yourself: "How deep and effective are the networks in the organization I lead?" Your answer will, in large part, tell you how healthy your enterprise is and how likely it is to thrive in the twenty-first-century economy. Networks are the future.

In short, networks are the new media — and medium — of success.

PARADIGM
2

Families Are the New Education

[F]amily, according to Rousseau, is "the most ancient of all societies and the only one that is natural...." Montaigne...criticizes the education of his day for aiming "at nothing but to furnish our heads with knowledge, but not a word of judgment and virtue."

—Mortimer Adler

John's example will have taught his children to go to school, get good grades, get a good job, work hard, "invest" in the retirement plan regularly; and as a result, be comfortable in retirement.

Terry's example will have taught her children that if they learn how to invest by starting small, to [build] their own business, and to keep their money working hard for them, they'll be rich....

My rich dad once asked me, "What's the difference between a person who bets on horses and one who picks stocks?"

"I don't know," was my response.

"Not much," was his answer. "Never be the person who buys the stock. What you want to be...is the person who creates the [business]."

—Robert Kiyosaki

Looking back through the history of education, it is interesting to note that it tends to mirror the trends of media rather closely. This isn't particularly surprising, since the whole point of media is to both reflect and, to a certain extent, *set* the cultural mindset.

> **Education is an extension of media in that it deals directly with the flow of ideas, understanding, and opinion in society.**

And in some ways, education is an extension of media in that it deals directly with the flow of ideas, understanding, and opinion in society. Looking at it from another angle, the media are an extension of education and even a type of education.

Naturally, since the trends of education and media have tended to shift and change together, much of what we say regarding both the past and future of education will look like the progression discussed in the previous chapter.

But the nuances that separate the two are deep and meaningful, and the way they appear in the distant past, as well as the developments and shifts we'll likely experience in the near future, give us a powerful picture of where education and media *should* be drastically different.

Education has the potential to adopt increased quality, leadership, and excellence in the way we approach learning in the decades ahead. To more deeply understand these trends, let's take a look at the nature and development of education.

From Ma's Lap to Pa's Fiddle

If we consider education 200 years ago, it looked very different from what has been typical over the past few decades, what we know as "normal" today. In fact, back then, almost every aspect of education ultimately started and ended with or in the family.

This isn't to say that everybody homeschooled but simply that the home was the central place of learning and education. When kids came home from school, parents and siblings were deeply involved in learning the most important lessons.

Family involvement in education wasn't limited to parents hounding children to complete homework and strictly discipline them when grades were less than satisfactory. On the contrary, many or most of the core values and ideas held by people in that era were learned on or near the laps of parents, aunts and uncles, grandparents, and older brothers and sisters.

> Many or most of the core values and ideas held by people 200 years ago were learned on or near the laps of parents, aunts and uncles, grandparents, and older brothers and sisters.

When the kids got home from school, and before they ever left in the morning, parents would sit down with them and make *sure* they were learning and understanding the most important lessons of life and also getting an academic education, whether the schools were teaching them or not.

A Reality

Actually, the way historians look at this is perhaps a little too calculated, too intentional, too premeditated — the result of trying to explain another era *during* a time (ours) when schooling is nearly always highly programmed. In fact, in early American homes, it wasn't the norm for parents to bring kids in from school and follow a specific checklist of topics or have their kids memorize the right answers.

Certainly there was an element of forethought in the way parents oversaw the education of their children, but even more than this was the *culture* of family learning that existed and influenced the education of children during that era.

In general, education on the most important topics came up naturally in the course of the evenings, not because parents necessarily sat down and planned what they wanted their young ones to know but because their culture included discussing the topics and ideas that mattered most to them on a regular basis and in all types of company, including near the small ears of children.

Parents daily talked with their children about the things they cared about, the things "everyone ought to know." They didn't always sit down to *teach* these things. Often it was less formal, not like the mechanics of a school.

The Little House

Family learning and education simply flowed from the moment as an organic absorption of principles. And it is important to note that literacy rates in that era were higher than today's literacy levels. (For example, in Boston, the literacy rate was approximately 85 percent in the years 1758–1762[7] and up to 90 percent between 1787 and 1795.[8] By 1800, the rate

> **Family learning and education simply flowed from the moment as an organic absorption of principles.**

was very close to 100 percent.[9] To compare, the literacy rate in Suffolk County, where Boston is found, was approximately 76 percent in 1992 and 75 percent in 2003.[10])

To get a feel for this eighteenth- and nineteenth-century culture of learning that was so widespread in America, consider the example of the Ingalls family in *Little House in the Big Woods*. At this point in the *Little House* series, the children were very young, and even if they had been old enough to attend school, the family didn't live near a school. But that is not the point of the book or the *reason* for the family culture of learning and the parental involvement in education.

Night after night, the reader sees Pa and Ma reading aloud to their children from the Bible and other classics, telling stories from their childhoods or family history, discussing ideas and principles, training in important skills, and ending the whole experience listening to Pa play on his fiddle and sing culturally significant songs.

By the time the children were school-aged, they were already steeped in a powerful culture of learning and education, and they knew their family's core beliefs and driving principles by heart. They also loved to learn. They were self-directed readers, thinkers, and studiers.

Interestingly enough, however, Laura Ingalls' series even further illustrates this point when, years later, the girls begin attending formal school and getting the majority of their academic training outside the home. Even when Pa and Ma start using outside help to supplement their home teaching, they are still highly involved in the daily educational journeys and successes of their children.

The local school is clearly only one important resource among many that make up the educational experience of the family's daughters, Laura and Mary.

Frankly, there are many books that allow us to witness and analyze this powerfully different approach to education. Reading old literature that discusses this period, such as the *Little House* series, the *Anne of Green Gables* series, the *Little Women* series, the *Little Britches* series, *Laddie*, *Understood Betsy*, and numerous others, can give us a peek into the old model of education, before the era of both mass media and expert-ruled public education.

Culture Trumps Lesson Plans

The important thing about this isn't that the learning happens somewhere other than school, since in each of these books powerful learning and educational progress happen through and with the aid of various types of schooling and formal education—both in the home and outside it.

Rather, the point is that the parents and family were actively involved in learning and took absolute responsibility for making sure upcoming generations learned the things that matter most and ultimately obtained a truly superb education.

This is deep! And, when read in fun stories like these, it is truly intriguing and even inspiring.

Of course, just as technology shifted the media, new advances and fluctuating world trends influenced educational systems and schooling approaches in the twentieth century.

From the Mouth of the Principal

Specifically, at the same time that people started relying more on experts for their media, they simultaneously started depending more on experts for education. People turned to certified teachers, credentialed professors, and textbooks targeted to specific fields and topics.

> At the same time that people started relying more on experts for their media, they simultaneously started depending more on experts for education.

Increasingly, families and even many churches gave way to school experts telling them what was right and what ideas they should know and believe in. Instead of teaching their children what they thought was best when they thought it was best, many began deferring to the suggestions of professional educators.

Over time, they looked to experts to tell them what jobs their children should engage in adult life, how they could best prepare for those jobs, and how they could qualify for and do them. Schools became less about life preparation and more focused on career training.

For some families, this new trend of education was actually a positive development. It meant greater opportunity to attend school, gain basic literacy, and work for higher levels of economic success. In previous systems, some families had very little chance of obtaining any education at all.

Unfortunately, while this system was good for some families, for many others, it actually meant decreased quality and excellence in education, not to mention the toll it took on the family itself. For too many families, the new educational model frequently meant decreased closeness and deteriorating relationships.

> For too many families, the new educational model frequently meant decreased closeness and deteriorating relationships.

Of course, as we've already discussed in the media chapter, the reliance on experts also meant a top-down control of ideas, thoughts, and overall cultural mindset, which naturally led to a societal decrease in freedom, depth, and understanding for many people.

As one author put it: "Freedom flourishes when the regular people have the same level of education and read the same books and ideas as their Senators, Governors, Presidents, Judges, and CEOs. When the leaders have a different level of education than the average person, the society is an aristocracy, pure and simple."[11]

Reliance on Experts

Over the past few decades, this trend has increased and deepened. People commonly rely on experts in the field of education to tell them what, when, and how to learn. More opportunity for specialized training for a greater number of people has coincided with a significant loss of deep, quality education for the people as a whole.

Fortunately, for those who desire a more open flow of ideas and learning options, the future is looking up. A new trend is gaining more weight and support in the world, one that looks an awful lot like the older pioneer system. With improvements in technology, every person has increased opportunities for both quality education and excellent career training.

> With improvements in technology, every person has increased opportunities for both quality education and excellent career training.

This brings us to the next paradigm shift: Families are the new education.

The New Fiddle

Again, this discussion is not meant simply to highlight the growing popularity of charter or alternative schools, online schooling programs, or homeschooling, though these are certainly a part of this trend. Rather, these developments are symptoms of a wider shift in education, wherein we see greater family involvement in learning at all levels.

While good parents have always tended to be involved in the education of their children, the types of involvement, and the *reasons* for involvement, are shifting. In the new world reality, educational, career, and even life success is increasingly built on the foundation of a strong family *culture* focused on learning.

> The new reality is also offering many of the perks, blessings, and opportunities that technology and social advancements have added over the past century.

But as mentioned above, the new reality is also offering many of the perks, blessings, and opportunities that technology and social advancements have added over the past century.

Specifically, in the new educational reality, a majority of parents still rely heavily on public or private institutions for the education of their children, but more and more people are starting to see teachers and administrators at such schools as guides who work for *the family,* as *their* paid employees, to provide the services *they* desire. This is a significant change.

The rise in popularity among parents of taking even more responsibility for the education of their children, for the sake of the education itself, is an important mark of the emerging paradigm.

The Problem with Balance

One of the great challenges of modern education is that it too often focuses on balance. Not the actual balance of putting everything in its best role and proper order, which is a good thing, but the definition of "balance" where uniformity, or even mediocrity, in five things is better than real excellence in one or two.

For example, a student who gets *B*s in math, science, history, and language arts is often considered more successful—in fact, smarter—than students who ignore subjects they don't care about and put all their effort into a great passion. They may dedicate themselves to becoming an excellent actor and getting a role on a TV program, focusing on the science fair and coming up with new technology that is purchased and developed in Silicon Valley, or winning a scholarship from billionaire Peter Thiel to quit school and start a powerful new innovation.

> One of the great challenges of modern education is that it too often focuses on balance.

Amazingly, in the old educational model, these three examples and others like them are considered failures by many educational professionals. "Stay in school," which was first introduced as a message to get high school dropouts to reconsider their choice, has in many circles become a mantra that is now applied to everyone, regardless of their other options.

Two Bad Assumptions

This is based on at least two faulty assumptions rampant in the old educational model. First is the idea that the *process* of schooling is the important thing, regardless of the result. In this view, even if students don't learn, if they in fact fall further behind each year, they should keep at it. Why? Just because "staying in school matters."

Granted, if the alternative is to join a gang, staying in school has its merit. However, staying in school is not the highest value intrinsically. There are those for whom staying in school would be a lesser educational path. Just consider the examples of Bill Gates, Michael Dell, Larry Page, Sergey Brin, and a number of others who all left college early to launch enormous companies.

> The old system rests on a belief that *schooling*, rather than learning, is the ultimate purpose.

Second, the old system rests on a belief that *schooling*, rather than learning, is the ultimate purpose. In this worldview, it is better to be in school and not learning than to be learning fabulously but not in school. Of course, this view directly benefits the job security of professional educators, but it does little to help students.

Both these myths—schooling before *learning* and schooling as *the only way* to learn—put the cart before the horse. As we will see in the next chapter, this is an even bigger problem at the college and university level than it is in K–12. But it is a negative wherever it appears.

The New Market

The purpose of schooling is learning. That's why schools were invented in the first place. And if a student can get better learning in some other way, he or she should likely do it. "Never let schooling get in the way of your education" is a better mantra than the old-style "Stay in school no matter what."

In the Information Age, education is more important than ever. As the global economy increases competition for jobs as well as competition for business success (for owners, not employees) to a worldwide market, learning is rising in value. But not rote learning and assembly-line obedience. These modalities are decreasing in marketability.

> The purpose of schooling is learning. That's why schools were invented in the first place. And if a student can get better learning in some other way, he or she should likely do it.

The new premium is on the ability to think independently and creatively, to take initiative and innovate, to lead, and to use ingenuity and tenacity to overcome challenges. These are the needed lessons of the new economy and therefore the ideal focus of today's educational curriculum.

Indeed, these bear repeating:

- The ability to think independently and creatively
- The ability to take initiative and innovate
- The ability to lead
- The ability to use ingenuity and tenacity to overcome challenges

Schools and students who flourish in these lessons will thrive in the twenty-first-century economy. Those who don't will fall behind.

The Right Balance

Thus, balance is being redefined in the new marketplace of business, jobs, and education.

For those who succeed in the emerging new system, balance will be seen as effectively excelling in at least three things at once:

1. Personal effectiveness and development and the ability to see and make needed personal changes
2. Proven leadership of others by building and growing teams that succeed
3. Excellence in marriage, family, and other close relationships

Again, laxity or mediocrity in any of these three is a recipe for failure in the new economy. Yet few schools are teaching *this* kind of balance or the skills for such excellence.

Parents must lead this trend. If they do, they'll help their children and youth get the kind of education that actually prospers in the new economy. The old kind of education simply isn't living up to the new realities of the job, career, or business market—not to mention the centrality of marriage and family leadership in long-term personal and career effectiveness.

If education wants to keep up and stay relevant, administrators and teachers—and especially parents—will need to refocus on the right kind of balance.

If education wants to keep up and stay relevant, administrators and teachers—and especially parents—will need to refocus on the right kind of balance, the kind where learning is king, skills are the central focus, and leadership is part of every lesson.

Toffler's Prediction

The old model isn't offering these results. As bestselling author Alvin Toffler put it:

> Built on the factory model, mass education taught basic reading, writing, and arithmetic, a bit of history and other subjects. This was the "overt curriculum."
>
> But beneath it lay an invisible or "covert curriculum" that was far more basic. It consisted—and still does in most industrial nations—of three courses: one in punctuality, one in obedience, and one in rote, repetitive work.[12]

This is exactly what factory jobs and many white-collar careers demand.

Some educators wanted to be sure that this model would last, so they designed modern schooling with this in mind. "To prepare youth for the job market," Toffler wrote, "educators designed standardized curricula. Men like Binet and Terman devised standardized intelligence tests. School grading policies, admission procedures, and accreditation rules were similarly standardized. The multiple-choice test came into its own."[13]

> The needs of the economy have now changed, and what young people need from their education in order to succeed in the current market is drastically different from what it was even ten years ago.

These all buttressed the old model: preparing prompt, obedient workers to perform in rote, repetitive tasks. And the current mainstream educational system still follows this pattern.

But the needs of the economy have now changed, and what young people need from their education in order to succeed in the current market is drastically different from what it was even ten years ago. Sadly, most schools haven't significantly changed with the times.

Again, parents must lead out — or watch their youth fall behind along with the old schooling model. They need to help their children seek the kind of education that will flourish in the twenty-first-century economy. In Toffler's words, today's young people need to learn to be:

- "less pre-programmed and faster on their feet"
- "complex, individualistic, proud of the ways in which they differ from other people"
- hungrier for increased responsibility[14]

Those who succeed in the new economy need to "get off the conveyor belt," as Oliver DeMille put it, "and become the leaders they were born to be."[15] They need to, as taught by Chris Brady, embrace their inner Rascal.[16] To do this, they need to truly be themselves, find their life purpose, and go after it.

The Banker and the Rascal

In the nineteenth-century classic *The Birth of Tragedy*, Friedrich Nietzsche argued that there are two main forces in society. First is what he called the Apollonian, which is "measured, balanced, rational, imbued with reason and self-restraint."[17] The second is the Dionysian, which is "wild, untamed, hard to understand, emerging from the inner layers of ourselves."[18]

The battle between these two forces, Nietzsche said, is the ongoing struggle of history. Beyond Nietzsche's commentary, this same challenge is a major life experience for each individual person.

And it is central to education. Some educational systems (like the training of young Spartans, Mongols, and Vikings, for example) emphasized preparing the youth to almost exclusively use their wild, untamed side. This led to warlike nations of conquest and empire.

Other educational models emphasized a nearly sole focus on the lessons of order, self-restraint, and fitting in, such as nineteenth-century Britain, twentieth-century America, and post-1950 Japan. This "buttoned-down" approach is epitomized in art and film by the characters of the Banker and the Accountant.

Flying a Kite

Which brings us to *Mary Poppins*. This Disney movie is, of course, one of the great classics on the topic of education, and it gets to the heart of "the Banker versus the Rascal."

In this movie, the Rascal, Mary Poppins, helps the Banker get past his ridiculous and unloving approach to his family and become a better father by finding his wilder side. While flying a kite might not be everyone's idea of really loosening up and "getting a life," for Mr. Banks, it was downright revolutionary.

Indeed, many if not most modern movies and television programs show the struggles between the Apollonian and the Dionysian—or, because they're easier to remember, the Banker and the Rascal. We all have both personalities inside, and we must choose when and where, and to what degree, to let them out.

The key is to use both. Sometimes we need to be ordered, rational, and prudent; other times, we need to go with our heart and be a maverick. The modern American educational emphasis on always putting the Banker above the Rascal is a serious flaw, which has caused numerous problems for people trying to navigate our current schooling/career system.

Put simply, if young people don't educate their Rascal, they aren't really educated. And they won't achieve greatness—because most of them won't even try. Aiming for greatness is a Rascal trait. All of us are capable of it, but modern education has downplayed this inner striving.

> **Put simply, if young people don't educate their Rascal, they aren't really educated.**

Ancient Rascals

This theme isn't limited to modern cinema or educational systems; it also runs through the classic literature of history. For example, Shakespeare's leading characters spend much of their time dealing with this exact question.

When Hamlet asks, "To be or not to be?" he is grappling with this very dilemma.

In essence, he's asking himself: "Should I follow the normal role of a grieving son with decorum and submit to the system imposed by the new king? Or should I go with my heart and stop this charade that the new king is forcing upon us?"

The same tension animates two of the greatest figures of ancient Greek drama: Oedipus and Antigone. Both of these characters must choose between the "buttoned-down system of fitting in (Banker style)" and "going for what I really feel in my heart (Go, Rascal! Go!)."

This is precisely where we are as a society today. From 1945 to very recently, the "Banker" approach has dominated our culture. A few "Rascals" such as Steve Jobs, Bill Gates, Mark Zuckerberg, Elon Musk, and others like them have made huge contributions to technology, leadership, and progress, but the masses have found most of their career success by following the "good grades/good job/good promotions" model.

With a high-growth middle-class economy, this system worked for over five decades. But with the rise of a much more competitive global marketplace, the rough-and-tumble economy of the twenty-first century is no longer built this way. It demands different skills and a different kind of leader (and, therefore, a different kind of education).

As a result, the old-style educational model is increasingly outdated and archaic. And this trend is only going to accelerate.

Parents Must Lead

If parents depend on outdated education models to prepare their youth for the careers of the new economy, they're going to witness a major decline in the next generation's standard of living. Those who excel in the rising global marketplace will be the Rascals, the innovators, those who learn how to compete in the new economy.

This is the call of education today. And since few schools are rising to this new standard (education is notorious for being one of the last sectors in society to adapt), parents and leaders who want to help the rising generation excel will need to realize this and help lead a true paradigm shift in education.

Of course, it's important not to go too far in either extreme because both the Banker and the Rascal have a part to play. But in our modern society, we've gone far too far toward the Banker. We need to refocus on the Rascal to rekindle North America's leadership, innovative, and business edge.

> **In short: Families are the new education or, at least, the new educational leaders.**

And education must be a key part of this.

Those who don't embrace this change could easily fall behind. Remember, true leaders see what really is and take action accordingly.

> **If your family actively embraces the new situation and leads out, you will seek effective ways to help your youth flourish in the new educational imperatives of the twenty-first century.**

In short: Families are the new education or, at least, the new educational leaders. If your family actively embraces the new situation and leads out, you will seek effective ways to help your youth flourish in the new educational imperatives of the twenty-first century.

It's time for your family to think Rascal.

PARADIGM
3

Mentors Are the New College

Study hard so you can find the right business to buy.
—ROBERT KIYOSAKI

Students starting school this year may be part of the last generation for which "going to college" means packing up, getting a dorm room and listening to tenured professors. Undergraduate education is on the verge of a radical reordering. Colleges, like newspapers, will be torn apart by new ways of sharing information enabled by the Internet. The business model that sustained private U.S. colleges cannot survive.

—ZEPHYR TEACHOUT, *THE WASHINGTON POST*

A study of the history and future of education quite naturally leads to the question of what college was, is, and will be. In a world where college seems to many people a necessary rite of passage for all who ultimately hope to be successful, understanding past and present college-related trends will prove illuminating to leaders who hope to understand where the future of higher learning is headed.

Success as It Was

What might surprise many people living in modern times is the simple but true fact that throughout most of the history of the world, only a small percentage of society actually went to college.

Until the middle of the twentieth century, college was reserved almost solely for future teachers and the children of the aristocracy. If you didn't plan on teaching, or your family didn't have a lot of money and a high position in society, it was very unlikely you'd ever go to any "institution of higher learning." And, what's more shocking to those who grew up after World War II, not attending college *didn't* reflect poorly on you as an individual.

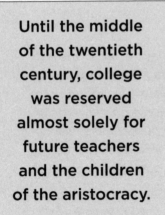

Until the middle of the twentieth century, college was reserved almost solely for future teachers and the children of the aristocracy.

If you did go to college, good for you! But for the vast majority of people—those who didn't—not having done so didn't make them losers, failures, deadbeats, or any other type of disgrace in the eyes of their parents or grandparents. Moreover, those who did attend went primarily to study the greatest classics in human history, to learn to think more deeply, and to better prepare themselves to make a meaningful contribution to society.

Of course, there were other opportunities for doing these things, and while many hoped to go to college, others preferred a different approach and consequently took a different path to their particular goals for success.

When many elites sent their children to college, they weren't expecting the school to provide a specific means of employment to its graduates but rather, as author William Deresiewicz noted, to teach them how to think creatively and critically and how to find a sense of and passion for their unique life purpose.

Many aspiring teachers went for the same reasons and hoped to learn the skills that would enable them to pass on similar enlightenment to the young pupils they'd have charge of in their chosen field in the classroom.

The Historical Record

Studying old literature, such as the *Anne of Green Gables* series, *Little Women, The Virginian,* and other such classics, gives us a better idea of what college meant to most ordinary people—an opportunity for some and an important part of many a teacher's education. To repeat: Those who didn't go could still be highly successful adults and citizens in society. And for those who did, the focus was firmly set in classics and life purpose.

> Those who didn't go to college could still be highly successful adults and citizens in society. And for those who did, the focus was firmly set in classics and life purpose.

Similarly, studying old literature of aristocratic societies, such as the writings of Jane Austen and Charles Dickens and many of Shakespeare's works, we see relevant examples of what college meant to them. For aristocrats, university was often important and expected, but in their case, it was even more about digging into history's greatest thinkers and ideas, learning to think in powerful ways, and preparing to become a more impactful and influential member of the aristocracy and society as a whole.

The GI Bill

Clearly there were many who desired to participate in college learning but were held back by finances, situation, or circumstance. The end of World War II brought a huge influx of young adults who felt a drive to find purpose through the type of organized communities and programs offered by colleges (more, in fact, than ever before in one place at one time in recorded history), and the world shifted in an interesting way in order to accommodate this new generation's needs.

The US government offered the GI Bill, which paid for college for many returning military personnel. This created a culture of many in the masses attending institutions of higher learning, and the economy simultaneously shifted to a new era of increased opportunity for "white collar" employment. Like college, before this point in history, only a very few had participated in white-collar careers. After this shift, a much larger segment of society joined the ranks of those employed in suit-and-tie work.

The Organization Man

This major change in the organization of society was described in 1956 by a groundbreaking book penned by William Whyte and entitled *The Organization Man*. Whyte argued that a new ethos and a new energy had overtaken America in the decade beginning in 1945.

This new perspective replaced the old prevailing notion of American "rugged individualism" with a new "collectivistic ethic."[19] In other words, the new mass migration to college and white-collar careers changed the American Dream from that of what Chris Brady called the Rascal to that of the Banker.

As one review of Whyte's classic study put it:

> A key point was made that people became convinced that organizations and groups could make better decisions than individuals, and thus serving an organization became logically preferable to advancing one's individual creativity....[T]his system led to risk-averse executives who faced no consequences and could expect jobs for life as long as they made no egregious missteps.[20]

Another bestseller in this era, the novel by Sloan Wilson entitled *The Man in the Gray Flannel Suit*, similarly argued that "those Americans inspired to win World War II returned to an empty suburban life, conformity, and the pursuit of the dollar."[21]

While critics responded that such a life wasn't exactly empty and that supporting one's family is an excellent pursuit, the core of the message stuck: a whole generation of Americans stopped seeking the old American Dream of business ownership and started working for the growth and goals of somebody else's corporation.

> A whole generation of Americans stopped seeking the old American Dream of business ownership and started working for the growth and goals of somebody else's corporation.

This was a massive change indeed. Another review of Whyte's classic book summarized the period this way:

It is life under the protection of the big organization—the corporation, the government, perhaps the university, charitable organization, or labor union. Here modern Americans find the jobs that promise security and a high standard of living, and, Mr. Whyte believes, give up the hopes and ambitions that dominated earlier generations of Americans.[22]

A perusal of some of the chapter titles in Whyte's famous book outline the key trends of this shift in American society. For example:

- Chapter 2: The Decline of the Protestant Ethic
- Chapter 6: A Generation of Bureaucrats
- Chapter 7: The Practical Curriculum
- Chapter 14: How Good an Organization Man Are You?
- Chapter 15: The Tests of Conformity
- Chapter 16: The Fight Against Genius

- Chapter 24: Inconspicuous Consumption
- Chapter 28: The Organization Children
- Appendix: How to Cheat on Personality Tests

Whyte clearly had deep concerns about this major change to America, one dominated by spending childhood and youth preparing for college, using college almost exclusively to prepare for employment, and then spending your life working for a big organization instead of your own business dreams. He considered this a step down, not a step up, for our national progress.

College Changes

But perhaps Whyte's most telling argument came in chapter eight, titled "Business Influence on Education." As mentioned, in 1944, the Servicemen's Readjustment Act (more commonly known as the GI Bill) passed, granting numerous benefits to World War II veterans, including significant government aid for college attendance.

> **Gradually at first and then with increasing swiftness, colleges became less classics-/thinking-/mission-oriented and became more focused on training students for specific jobs and career fields.**

Once this legislation was adopted, literally millions of people chose to go to college who would otherwise have gone in different directions. This huge change was naturally accompanied by a shift in what college was all about and what it even offered.

Gradually at first and then with increasing swiftness, colleges became less classics-/thinking-/mission-oriented and became more focused on training students for specific jobs and career fields. More people started attending colleges as the decades flew by, and colleges increasingly concentrated on providing students with career skills designed to make them more employable in large organizations.

Where college had once been an immersion in great authors, important ideas, and profound classics, designed to teach real and deep thinking, it turned into a rush to get "general education" out of the way and train individuals with the "useful" abilities they'd need to "succeed in the real world."

Again, the old idea of college was to help individuals define who they were and were meant to be, then to help them learn how to reach their best ideals and goals, and then to send them off to do it. In contrast, the new idea was simply to teach them to do something that would bring a living wage in the growing postwar Corporate-Government Establishment.

> **Society was increasingly inclined to the new idea that college was necessary to success itself.**

Of course, as more and more people went to college to prepare for this path and were then told they had obtained success once they were working for a big organization, society was increasingly inclined to the new idea that college was necessary to success itself.

The Ivy-Washington Establishment

By the mid-1960s, and certainly by the early 1980s, most middle-class families in North America had latched on to a societal tradition of college — a culture where college was expected for most of the highly compensated jobs and careers.

In this era, more people had the opportunity to go to college than ever before in history, and at the same time, those who didn't have a college degree were less likely to get the best organization jobs. Many employers grew significantly less likely to select non–college graduates for jobs or projects than their "well-educated" counterparts.

In some fields, such as medicine, law, and some fields of technology, this made practical sense. Naturally, when you went to have your leg operated on, you wanted someone who had been trained to do it right! It's also true that a lawyer who didn't know the law would be less than ideal, and a person who couldn't build a rocket shouldn't be hired for such a task.

In occupations where there is a very specific right and wrong way to learn and do things, there is merit in having a clearly defined training program and even a uniform system of credentials. In other arenas, this model made less sense because there was little correlation, if any, between the training offered by college courses and the actual skills and abilities needed to truly succeed and excel.

The idea behind this general societal shift was that a person with a college education would have broader understanding and education. Of course, as the system continued to move further down the path it chose in 1944, this focus grew less likely to produce the results it intended, and mediocre outcomes multiplied.

> **The idea behind this general societal shift was that a person with a college education would have broader understanding and education.**

Over time, by attempting to make everyone broadly educated, college more often succeeded only in making people randomly or even trivially educated in the "general" subjects. This neither helped them focus effectively in their chosen career or life mission nor made them well-rounded or deeply educated.

At the same time, with increasing government regulation and red tape, the price of college tuition skyrocketed. To top it off, as the decades passed, the number of college graduates who couldn't get a job in their chosen field — or even one related to their college studies — increased.

> **As the decades passed, the number of college graduates who couldn't get a job in their chosen field—or even one related to their college studies—increased.**

By 2010, only 62.1 percent of graduates were employed in a job that required a degree, and only about 27.3 percent worked in a field related to their major.[23] Outside of medicine, law, technology, and education, the percentage is even smaller.

Another Major Shift

We are now witnessing yet another momentous change in the college/career/business environment. Two major developments—the decreasing effectiveness of a college education in securing employment for its graduates and the advent and universality of the Internet—have recently shifted everything.

The Internet has changed what is even possible in education, and the higher-price/lower-value aspect of college itself has spurred a fresh crop of books and articles discussing the advent of a whole new era of higher education. This change is as significant as when the GI Bill launched the postwar system many decades ago.

For instance, in his 2015 book *College (Un)bound,* author Jeffrey J. Selingo outlined several disruptive forces that are drastically changing higher education and will continue to do so in the years and decades ahead. These include:

1. "The Sea of Red Ink." This refers to the near-endless amount of paperwork, regulation, red tape, and oversight that colleges have to deal with nowadays. Because of reams of regulations passed since 1944 that mandate all kinds of restrictions, management practices, and other behaviors for colleges,

this is a huge business—and it has little to do with education.

Because of these many added aspects of administration, and the fact that they're governmentally mandated and legally required, the amount of money colleges have to dedicate to administrative costs alone has expanded far beyond what it should be. This one issue alone adds massive costs to getting a college degree, and it is one that is unlikely to change anytime soon.

Again, the fact that it's all legally enforced naturally means the leaders must shift their focus from education to administration. This increases the price colleges have to charge for tuition and also ties their hands in terms of who they can accept, who they can hire, what they can teach, and how they run their whole institution. This "Sea of Red Ink" makes the price of college extremely high for prospective students, and they aren't paying more for higher quality educational opportunities or experiences. Instead, as mentioned, they're paying merely to afford the myriad administrators, lawyers, consultants, staffers, and others who never actually add specific value to any individual's education or personal learning.

> **The fact that many added aspects of administration are legally enforced naturally means the leaders must shift their focus from education to administration.**

At the same time, growing regulation and restrictions are making it harder and harder for those who do have a hand in real education to teach the things that truly matter. Accreditation bureaucracies have added myriad private regulations to those already enforced by governments.

"Simply put, many Americans fail to finish college, because many colleges are not designed to be finished. They are designed to enroll students, yes. They are built to garner research funds and accrue status through rankings and the scholarly articles published by faculty. But those things have little to do with making sure students leave prepared to thrive in the modern economy."[24]

2. "The Disappearing State." Selingo also explains that when college first became the central part of young adult society we today consider it to be, it was built largely on government funding. Unfortunately for those who want a similar experience to what was offered in the mid to late twentieth century, the recession of 2008 and 2009 brought with it a huge decrease in what governments are willing to spend on college.

Indeed, the "college bubble" came right after the housing bubble burst in 2008, causing the Great Recession. Free market theorists applauded the end of a system where most students who went to college did so only because they were subsidized by Washington. This exposed the reality that college wasn't a national birthright, forcing many people to rethink their view of higher education in the emerging new economy.

As government gives less to and requires more from colleges, the students themselves or their families are left to make up the difference by paying more. Yet, as discussed in the section on the growing "Sea of Red Ink," their money mostly goes to administrators and bureaucrats who have little or nothing to do with the quality of learning students receive.

> As government gives less to and requires more from colleges, the students themselves or their families are left to make up the difference by paying more.

At the same time, the quality of many college and university educational offerings, majors, and programs are in question—and also in decline.

Many educators—who owe their careers to the old postwar educational system and who love the university culture that peaked from the 1950s to the 2000s—are worried that few schools even see quality education as their main goal or purpose anymore. More on this below.

3. "The Well of Full-Paying Students Is Running Dry." This third challenge is exactly what it sounds like. A huge percentage of students at college have their tuition and costs at least partially funded

by government aid. As the government pays less for students, many are finding other things to do with their post-high-school years. Future "college bubbles" are expected as this trend deepens.

4. "The Unbundled Options Are Improving." This is perhaps one of the most important points Selingo teaches because it goes beyond outlining the shortcomings or mistakes of the modern college bureaucracy and actually discusses some alternatives to college that offer everything college was originally *meant* to provide.

    With the advent of the Internet, a number of new "unbundled" college-level learning options are widely available. In essence, "unbundled education" focuses on learning rather than credits, general ed requirements, majors, degrees, or credentials. The unbundled revolution is based on the idea that in the increasingly competitive global marketplace, it is quality education, knowledge, skills, creativity, innovation, and leadership that matter.

    This changes everything, just as much as the GI Bill altered higher education in the 1940s. With quality skills, creativity, innovation, and leadership as the focus of learning, the old-style reliance on college credentials is rapidly losing value.

    Unbundled options can still intersect with traditional university requirements, such as earning credit in online or community college courses, supplemented by a few night classes, and transferring them all to your school of choice. But increasingly, the unbundled revolution also suggests forgoing formal college measures (such as credit and degrees) and instead focusing on quality education—knowledge and skills that bring success in the new economy. Again, this is as big a shift as Whyte's Organization Man and the GI Bill but in the opposite direction—toward individualism rather than collectivism.

The result is a growing number of young people—and even a significant number of their parents—who are looking for success outside the "big university/big corporation" tent. In all this, entrepreneurialism is growing in popularity. The impact on education is drastic, and it will only increase in the years and decades ahead.

Two Types of Unbundling: Mild vs. Hot

As mentioned, a "mild" level of unbundling occurs by giving students more opportunities to obtain college credit and work toward graduation. Where the old model of college was to spend four (and often five) years on campus attending classes, participating in the various social and extracurricular programs, and progressing to graduation, the unbundling revolution is based on the following main opportunities:

1. Taking community college courses during high school years and getting ahead before attending college
2. Living at home during college-age years and taking local college courses
3. Participating in online classes to earn college credit
4. Attending night and other alternative schedule coursework
5. Earning credits from a combination of options 1–4 above and bundling them at one college, along with a few on-site classes (for a semester or two), to meet graduation requirements

On the other hand, a less mild effect of the unbundling revolution is that more people are forgoing official college and simply seeking a great education in other ways. When college credit isn't the goal and becoming effective and thriving in the real economy is the driving focus, a number of additional alternatives are available to those seeking quality education. For example:

> **When college credit isn't the goal and becoming effective and thriving in the real economy is the driving focus, a number of additional alternatives are available to those seeking quality education.**

6. Taking classes from one or many of the new, often free Internet educational options. One such offering is Khan Academy, which provides classes on numerous topics from beginning to advanced levels.

   Udacity is a similar program, offering various college-level classes. Indeed, Udacity emphasizes what it calls the "Nanodegree," a set of courses that allow you to gain mastery of new skills needed for a specific field. All online, of course.

   The online Coursera program allows students to take multiple classes from some of the best professors in the world. For example, you can simultaneously enroll in a Princeton University course on algorithms, a University of Michigan class on successful negotiation, a Duke University course on English composition, and a Peking University class on Chinese for beginners. Indeed, from their own homes, students can scroll through numerous offerings for the next two months and design their own courses of study.

   Another example: for the next few weeks, you can take a Tel Aviv University class on economic growth and distributive justice, a World Bank Group course on private-public partnerships, a Georgia Institute of Technology class on control of mobile robots, a University of Hong Kong course on understanding China, and a Stanford University class on surveillance law.

7. Or people can altogether dispense with university-style courses and just go after superb knowledge. A number of young people are finding that the best way to get a truly quality education in their field of interest is to apprentice with a top leader in that discipline.

In fact, in a world where a degree is less valuable than your street cred and real learning, a lot of people are wondering why structured college is needed. A college-level *education* is incredibly valuable, but the traditional campus is only one possible source and is often inferior to the many alternatives available.

If learning is the focus — and it is — then colleges are often holding students back. For many young people and adults, there are simply better ways to get college-level learning.

For example, PayPal cofounder and billionaire Peter Thiel made headlines when he offered $100,000 to young people who would skip or leave college and go build something that matters. In its first few years, participants "have produced more than $200 million in economic activity, including revenue, investments…and grants.

"They have started 58 organizations that employ more than 200 people and create new technologies that are being deployed around the world. Organizations started by [them] have an aggregate value of more than half a billion dollars."[25]

That's quite a way to spend your college years. And note that the Thiel program typically lasts two years, not four. Of course, participants frequently use these two years to launch projects that last much longer and keep them busily engaged for years to come.

> **Internships, apprenticeships, and business start-ups are just a few of the alternatives young people have for getting a superb education that really prepares them to thrive in the new economy.**

Internships, apprenticeships, and business start-ups are just a few of the alternatives young people have for getting a superb education that really prepares them to thrive in the new economy. There are a number of exciting learning programs that help launch young people on such a leadership path, including Breakout Labs, Enstitute, Mass Challenge, Life Leadership, the Center for Social Leadership, and UnCollege.

Because the unbundling revolution is still in its infancy, many such organizations will be launched and grow in the decade ahead.

8. Another top-rate, cutting-edge way to get a superb education is to find a mentor, make an arrangement to learn from him or her, and get to work on whatever the mentor assigns. Actually, this is the way most lawyers and doctors learned before the era of assembly-line schooling, and it is still one of the

very best educational models available for many fields.

While one can't currently become a doctor or attorney in most places using this approach, direct mentoring can be one of the most effective ways to get an excellent education. Seek out mentors who are leaders in the field you want to excel in yourself, and approach them about mentoring you. Make a list of possible top mentors, and keep working at it until one of them agrees

> One top-rate, cutting-edge way to get a superb education is to find a mentor, make an arrangement to learn from him or her, and get to work on whatever the mentor assigns.

to help you. Then work very hard to get the education he or she prescribes.

Life Leadership is one example of an organization that combines such one-on-one mentoring with focused reading, audios, and live lectures, hands-on entrepreneurship, and other real-world learning.

Note that in practice, the one-on-one mentoring method is often a challenging path to a great education, since top mentors are frequently very demanding, but the results are usually worth the extra effort. If you work with the right mentor, there is no better way to get a truly quality education.

In short, mentoring is the new college—whether you work one-on-one with a top mentor in your chosen field or with a program like the Thiel Fellowship, a Life Leadership mentor, or a wise guide who helps you find and get the courses you want and the learning you need in a combination of online, life-experience, on-campus, and other studies and projects.

9. Finally, in the Information Age, some young people are simply ignoring the old system, with its bureaucracies and requirement checklists, and instead going after their own educational experience. They seek out training videos or tutorials on YouTube and learn important information and skills. They listen to TED talks; read various books, periodicals, websites, and blogs that teach myriad subjects; and dig in to learn, learn, learn.

   Those who use this model will find their efforts more effective if they work with a wise, experienced mentor who can help guide such learning. Without a mentor, an Information Age learning approach is often just that—information.

   But to thrive in the new economy, it is essential to go beyond information and add skills, focus, real-life experience, and application. This is much more effective when you have the benefit of depth and wisdom that a good mentor can provide. Parents can often fill this role for youth or help young adults seek out the right mentors.

It's Becoming Common Knowledge

College (Un)bound isn't the only recent work outlining important shifts in the new college/career world. Colleges and universities, along with their potential students, are facing a growing value gap—where the price of college is going up while the value of a degree is going down for many students in the real-world market.

Other challenges to the old college model include what Selingo called "the great credential race," "the lack of personalized education," and the reality that some of the most important skills necessary to success in the current economy have nothing to do with schooling! In fact, in many cases, schooling is reducing rather than increasing these skills (such as innovation, initiative, self-directed leadership, agility under pressure, and creativity).

> **Quality learning and real education in knowledge and skills at the college level, or beyond, is more valuable than ever, but for an increasing number of people, college isn't providing these things.**

Quality learning and real education in knowledge and skills at the college level, or beyond, is more valuable than ever, but for an increasing number of people, college isn't providing these things.

As an overview of Glenn Harlan Reynolds' book *The Higher Education Bubble* put it:

America is facing a higher education bubble. Like the housing bubble, it is the product of cheap credit coupled with popular expectations of ever-increasing returns on investment, and as with housing prices, the cheap credit has caused college tuitions to vastly outpace inflation and family incomes. Now this bubble is bursting....

Reynolds explains the causes and effects of this bubble and the steps colleges and universities must take to ensure their survival. Many graduates are unable to secure employment sufficient to pay off their loans, which are usually not dischargeable in bankruptcy. As students become less willing to incur debt for education, colleges and universities will have to adapt to a new world of cost pressures and declining public support.[26]

Or as Andrew Delbanco noted in the book *College: What It Was, Is, and Should Be:* "As the commercialization of American higher education accelerates, more and more students are coming to college with the narrow aim of obtaining a preprofessional credential." College isn't what it used to be for many students, and today it is often just a ticket-punching exercise for those who want to get into law, dental, or medical schools.

This is a major development. Given the current legal structure of medical and attorney licensing as well as contemporary law and medical school entrance requirements, the undergraduate college experience is necessary for those who want to enter these professions. But if this becomes a main focus of colleges, these requirements are likely to change.

Delbanco argues that college should be much more than this, suggesting that a great education for all is very important for our national survival. In terms almost reminiscent of Allan Bloom's *The Closing of the American Mind,* he recommends that colleges make serious changes. Until they do, however, the current devaluing of college will likely continue.

> **College isn't what it used to be for many students, and today it is often just a ticket-punching exercise for those who want to get into law, dental, or medical schools.**

A Deluge of Testimony

In all this torrent of commentary on the changes to the economy and higher education, there are two major types of books that chronicle the challenges of North American universities. One type suggests fixing colleges, and the other recommends moving on to better systems of learning using various unbundled options. But—tellingly—both argue that the era of "career training colleges and Organization Man careers" for the middle class is or soon will be over.

In a 2015 book by Kevin Carey, the title says it all: *The End of College: Creating the Future of Learning and the University of Everywhere.* Instead of emphasizing the phrase "unbundled revolution," Carey focuses on what he calls "MOOCs," or "massive open online courses."

This is a major revolution indeed. Carey wrote: "The trustees at the University of Virginia went so far as to abruptly fire their recently hired president for insufficient entrepreneurialism after reading an op-ed in the *Wall Street Journal* about MOOCs....Virginia eventually hired their president back after being denounced by the press. But the die was cast...."[27]

When a major university fires its president for "insufficient entrepreneurialism," we are living in a very different world and economy than the 1945–2005 era of big business/big university domination.

The point is simple. Whatever you call this altered reality, from "unbundled" or "MOOCs" to "the new economy" or "mentors are the new college," we are now entering a different epoch in education, one where what Carey called the "University of Everywhere" is king. The reality is...reality.

Counting Sheep

In perhaps the most controversial book on higher education since *The Closing of the American Mind*, former Yale professor and bestselling author William Deresiewicz's 2015 work *Excellent Sheep* argued that "our nation's top schools should be—but aren't—providing" a truly quality education.[28]

Deresiewicz lamented that his former Ivy League "students, some of the nation's brightest minds, were adrift when it came to the big questions: how to think critically and creatively and how to find a sense of purpose."[29]

As a result of this development, he warned, "elite colleges are turning out conformists without a compass."[30]

They aren't training our leaders, as most people believe, but rather consistently molding the "best and brightest" into followers—or, to use Deresiewicz's word, "sheep."

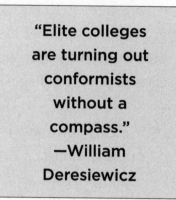

"Elite colleges are turning out conformists without a compass."
—William Deresiewicz

And there are an increasing number of such commentaries. For example, in the 2015 book *College Disrupted: The Great Unbundling of Higher Education*, Ryan Craig shows that with "the advent of…'MOOCs'… predictions that higher education will be the next industry to undergo 'disruption' have become more frequent and fervent.

"Currently a university's reputation relies heavily on the 'four R's' in which the most elite schools thrive—rankings, research, real estate, and rah! (i.e., sports). But for the majority of students who are not attending these elite institutions, the 'four R's' offer poor value for the expense of a college education."[31]

With the proliferation of vocal warnings that this shift is occurring, almost everyone in the education profession realizes that major changes are afoot in higher education—and that the college and university degree system's long-term survival is at stake.

The Deaf Ear

Ironically, however, the one segment of the population that seems oblivious to these widely discussed developments is middle-class parents of college-age or soon-to-be college-age students. Perhaps this is understandable, given the traditional viewpoint of how college has benefited the middle class since 1945. Indeed, for many middle-class families, college is an essential rite of passage — regardless of the fact that the "four R's" have largely taken over many, even most, undergraduate campuses.

> For many middle-class families, college is an essential rite of passage.

Sadly, as a result, many students this year and in the decade ahead won't even be given the opportunity to seriously consider the nine quality alternatives to four-year on-campus schooling listed above.

Leaders realize, however, that most such perceptions are merely perceptions, not reality. Even for students who do attend college — to qualify for law or medical schools, for example, or to earn their teaching credential, or to (in the old style of the upper classes) get a great classical education — mentoring is vital. College students with good mentors tend to flourish, while others frequently learn much less.

> For everyone — whether on campus or off — mentoring is the new college.

For everyone—whether on campus or off—mentoring is the new college. And likewise, mentoring is usually the most important key to great learning.

More Voices

An additional book on the topic provides a powerful insight. Former US Secretary of Education William J. Bennett's 2013 book *Is College Worth It?* outlines and prescribes solutions for what he calls "the broken promise of higher education."

Secretary Bennett tackles the topic head on. As the marketing ad to his book put it:

> For many students, a bachelor's degree is considered the golden ticket to a more financially and intellectually fulfilling life. But the disturbing reality is that debt, unemployment, and politically charged pseudo learning are more likely outcomes for many college students today than full-time employment and time-honored knowledge.
>
> This raises the question: is college still worth it? Who is responsible for debt-saddled, undereducated students, and how do future generations of students avoid the same problems?

The answers to these questions are powerful, centering on the reality that today's young person (and parents, academic counselors, etc.) must take a personalized approach.

This is almost impossible to overstate. Personalization is that important in the current situation.[32]

In short: Personalize what is best for you, utilizing the various methods we've covered, for your dreams and goals, and work hard to get the education that will help get you where you want to be ten, twenty, and thirty years from now. This is different for different people and for different goals.

> Today's young person must take a personalized approach.

A mentor who has the kind of education, career, and/or results you want to emulate is extremely helpful in this process. With so many options and a rapidly changing educational playing field, a good mentor is essential to real success. As noted, the best mentors are already successful in your chosen field and in the ways you want to achieve.

Quality higher education is more important than ever — and it is available in a number of formats, both within official college circles and outside of them. Wherever it is found, one principle dominates: mentoring is the new college.

PARADIGM 4

Building a Business Is the New Career

We are shifting from a managerial society to an entrepreneurial society.

—John Naisbitt

Why do so many people today think that the American Dream is to get a job? To be an employee? That's not what this phrase originally meant. The American Dream was all about building a business, about owning your own company—about changing the world, and certainly your community, by the way you provided leadership in the enterprise(s) you owned. This was the cornerstone of free enterprise, the foundation of the American Dream. Any other definition is a step backwards, a symptom of modern decline.

—Oliver DeMille

We've already covered a number of themes that provide introduction for our fourth paradigm shift. The discussions of family life, education of children and youth, and higher education along with career training have outlined the fact that how the majority of people make a living in the new economy is undergoing significant changes.

To understand this shift, three additional thoughts are in order. First, as briefly mentioned earlier, while for the past three generations the best way for many people to get ahead financially was to go to a good school, get good grades, and graduate with a marketable degree, this is now true for fewer people.

Second, the new economy is much more competitive than that faced by young people trying to select and succeed in their careers between 1945 and 2005. This is a major change, one that the parents and grandparents of today's generation seem to find hard to believe. They typically have other explanations for the challenges faced by today's college-age and post-college-age young adults.

> Before 1945, few people prepared for their chosen careers in a college setting and then spent their entire adult lives working for the same company.

But the facts are the facts: we now live in a truly global economy, and the growth of the middle class has turned to negative growth in Europe and North America. The middle class—and corresponding middle-class jobs requiring college degrees and paying high wages along with good benefit packages—are now growing in Asia, not in the West.

Third, the postwar model of paid work is an anomaly in world history. Before 1945, few people prepared for their chosen careers in a college setting and then spent their entire adult lives working for the same company. This model is purely a 1945–2005 phenomenon, not a norm of history. It's not a tradition, not a general pattern, and certainly not an entitlement.

The Context of the Postwar Era

Between 1900 and 1945, upward class mobility was much less frequent. Tocqueville noted in *Democracy in America,* written in the 1830s, that the lower and middle classes in America had more opportunities for upward mobility than their counterparts in Europe and that a higher number of them took advantage of the freedoms and laws that encouraged entrepreneurialism.

The westward expansion beginning in the 1850s created additional opportunities for upward mobility. But by the 1900s, this had largely slowed. In all this, business ownership was the path to an improved family lifestyle. Some used such opportunities to better their situation — including many lower- and middle-class Americans and also immigrants from Asia, Latin America, and especially Europe.

Apart from business ownership, upward class mobility was rare. As mentioned, this changed in the aftermath of World War II. The rise of corporate opportunity and college training provided new options for a lot more people. A much larger percentage of traditionally lower-class youth used college to slingshot their way into the middle class, and many from the lower-middle class likewise turned four years on campus (and often a few more years in a professional school) into a step up to the middle-middle or upper-middle classes.

> **The rise of corporate opportunity and college training provided new options for a lot more people.**

Those already in the upper-middle class pushed their earning power and lifestyle to a much higher level, indeed surpassing the actual standard of living of historical aristocracies and members of the royal classes. The college/career model gained its popularity for a reason. The changes were real.

With that said, it is important to understand the full reality of what occurred. All of this happened in the course of a sixty-year growth economy during which North America became the leader of the free world, and the old leader—Europe—took decades to recover from a devastating war that left its cities widely demolished and its institutions and economies in tatters.

As the war ended in 1945, the United States had approximately 6 percent of the world's population but produced over half the world's goods and services. The result of this development, coupled with the rapid spread of industrialization and mass business and banking practices, all spurred by a shift of capital into North American ventures, was a long-term economic upswing. With growth came the opportunities for upward mobility outlined above, at a level unprecedented and to date unequaled in human history.

Today, a similar shift is happening, but this time, industry and capital are moving to Asia. This is a major change. Unlike in the 1940s, this is occurring without the drastic catalyst of war and destruction, so it is less noticeable to many people. But the changes are no less real.

The 80 Percent Clause

In all this, there is a hidden thread of success—unknown to the casual onlooker and unpublicized in most circles. We alluded to it earlier, but few people realize that this is the main story of America's sustained postwar economic rise. Those who do understand it realize that the transfer of the majority of the global middle class to Asia (and with it the many economic benefits that naturally follow) in the first third of the twenty-first century isn't a major disaster.

Not at all. But without this knowledge of what might be called the "80 Percent Clause," many Americans are deeply troubled by current economic downturn in the West and the simultaneous threat of a quickly rising Asian juggernaut. Most Americans are now concerned that their children and grandchildren won't have the same standard of living they have enjoyed, and they believe that the rising generations in China will have a better standard of living than their American peers.

But those who fully understand the 80 Percent Clause aren't troubled. It simply means that, through the postwar

American growth era, even during downturns such as those in the late 1970s or the Great Recession beginning in 2008, the driving force of economic growth was small business. It has been the entrepreneurs, family businesses, and founders/owners of small companies that have accounted for a large portion of real economic growth.[33]

> **It has been the entrepreneurs, family businesses, and founders/ owners of small companies that have accounted for a large portion of real economic growth.**

For example, as Thomas J. Stanley and William D. Danko found in their research for the bestselling book *The Millionaire Next Door*, over 80 percent of America's millionaires are self-made,[34] and two-thirds of America's millionaires are self-employed entrepreneurs building a business.[35]

> **This was the crux of the American Dream: making it big by building a business.**

This was the crux of the American Dream: making it big by building a business. The result of such success was that a lot of other people benefited along the way, thanks to the many jobs such ventures created. Any successful small business helps numerous people in the community and the nation. The dream of personal success in business ownership and the way it helps others is a central part of American history.

The small business sector generally relies less on traditional college training than big business and the corporations and more on the competitive values of initiative, innovation, ingenuity, tenacity, hard work, hungry stick-to-itiveness, and gutsy salesmanship. In short, the tools of success in the new economy are already part of the American ethos — but lodged in the entrepreneurial sector rather than the college/careerist part of the population.

Certainly the fact that less financial capital will be lodged in the West (because it is moving to Asia) is a major challenge, but this just increases the need for American ingenuity and innovation to again take center stage. How can we do it? This remains to be seen. That's why it's going to require ingenuity and innovation. But one thing is clear: this is a job for entrepreneurial leaders, and it's going to be led by those who once again put the American Dream of successful business ownership and cutting-edge personal leadership at the forefront.

> **Building a business is the new career, at least for those who want to not just survive but also flourish.**

Building a business is the new career, at least for those who want to not just survive but also flourish and lead in the more competitive market challenges of the rough-and-tumble new global economy. This is a battle for leaders.

It is also a turning point for America, Europe, and the West. We will either pass the baton of world and economic leadership to China and its neighbors, or we will innovate a new era of Western excellence.

It's up to us.

How to Thrive

The first step to becoming a more entrepreneurial society is to engage the concept of "antifragility."[36] The small business sector in America has proven to be very antifragile, in the words of Nassim Nicholas Taleb. Antifragile is the opposite of fragile, but it doesn't mean stable. It means better than stable.[37]

In other words, an antifragile sector of the economy does even better when difficult economic times come. Taleb compares antifragility to the Hydra from Greek mythology.[38] Cut off one of its heads, and it doesn't just survive. It grows back the head you cut off plus an additional head just to make things interesting. The more you hurt it, the stronger it gets.

Another key to increasing the entrepreneurialism of modern America is to clearly teach the next generation the truth—the difference between the old postwar economy and the new post–Great Recession global marketplace. One step, as Taleb puts it, is to help them realize "Commerce is natural, fun, thrilling, lively…[and] academia as currently professionalized is none of these."[39]

Young people seeking to be leaders should take a hard look at the power of entrepreneurship—in all career fields—to make a much bigger difference in the world, make a better living, and become effective and influential leaders.

The Risk Reality

A third way to engage entrepreneurial success yourself (and help spread a stronger entrepreneurial ethos in society) is to get serious about wise risk-taking. This is a key lesson that is seldom taught in modern schools — whether in K–12 classrooms or on campuses of higher learning.

The goal isn't risk for its own sake. It is success, service, achievement, and societal progress. But without risk, none of these happen. Also, not just any old risk will do. Real leaders know — or learn, often painfully — that *wise* risk is essential. It's still risk, yes. But wisdom is powerful, and it often makes a huge difference.

Taleb notes that America's "principal asset" is taking wise risks and being willing to succeed or failing and still trying anyway.[40] Those who do this are the ones columnist Ken Kurson called America's "steel-stomached small business people," who deal with crisis by finding ways to improve their business and expand even in the most difficult times.[41]

Too often, people on the conveyor belt college/career/promotion path listen to what Chris Brady called "the *Council of They.*" *They* are the thought police, the guardians of political correctness, the masters of conformity, the keepers of the status quo. It is *They* who struggle to keep life always the way *They* say it should be, who fight change, persecute creativity, and hurl criticism at anything that smacks of originality or authenticity.

They try to say who is "in" and who is "out." *They* seem to have so much power that good, creative people leave their lives on the shelf rather than face their wrath. *They* will try to influence how you live, what you do, whom you should marry, and how you should raise your children. *They* want control, obedience, and blind acquiescence....

The only problem is, that herd of people following along in step aren't going anywhere, and as long as anyone listens to them, he or she won't go anywhere either.[42]

The followers of *They* versus successful business ownership — this is the battle now. And the two are going in very different directions. Note that *They* are clearly caught in the old economy. Success in the new market belongs to those who push past the words, glances, and hollow promises of *They* to creatively innovate, build something that matters, and lead.

> **Success in the new market belongs to those who push past the words, glances, and hollow promises of *They* to creatively innovate, build something that matters, and lead.**

Indeed, this goes beyond the American Dream. Such independent leadership has long been the American Way.

The Team

So far, we've outlined three ways to go entrepreneurial, avoid the crash of the old, and lead out in the new economic realities. These include: 1) engaging antifragility and helping build it into your business, 2) spreading the message that entrepreneurialism is vital to success in the new system (and teaching this to our youth), and 3) learning how to thrive using wise risk.

A fourth key in this process is to join or build the right kind of team, one made up of individual leaders who are willing to do the hard work necessary for success—and to do it in cooperation with other leaders of this same bent. This is a powerful blend of independent thinking and synergy.

These are more than just catch phrases. They describe real traits that turn antifragility, entrepreneurialism, and wise risk into business success and growth. Leaders are only as effective as their team, and together they are a lot closer to greatness.

> **Leaders are only as effective as their team, and together they are a lot closer to greatness.**

As Toffler's research showed, the old model of economic success was based on the following:

- Standardization
- Specialization
- Synchronization
- Concentration

- Maximization
- Centralization

But the new economy demands a different worldview and a different approach by leaders focused on what Toffler called a "Small-Within-Big" mentality.[43] This means, simply, that some accomplishments are best achieved at the individual level, and nothing can take their place. If the individual doesn't do them, he or she won't achieve the desired success.

But that's only the start. Other tasks are most effectively accomplished at the small work-group level, say four to ten dedicated colleagues dreaming, planning, working, playing, and striving together for a shared set of exciting goals. This is where some of the most important work, including innovative breakthroughs and great accomplishments, occurs. Skip this level, and little really gets done.

Beyond this, there's the next level up, where three, four, or even a few more of these smaller units combine to challenge each other, compete, support, inspire, and at times even work together to push the whole project to a much higher level. This is profound. Malcolm Gladwell argued in *The Tipping Point* that such a group stops working well if it grows beyond 150 people, but up to that number, it can accomplish miracles.

> A full multitude of people working on the same goals and projects, made up of many cohorts, is a force of nature.

Beyond these three levels (the individual, the team, and the group), a cohort of teams and groups can create a revolution of success — much better together than apart. Again, however big the combination of cohorts gets, the individuals, small teams, and groups must keep thriving. But a full multitude of people working on the same goals and projects, made up of many cohorts, is a force of nature. If it desires, it is a force for good. It creates momentum, and the bigger and better it gets, the more strength it passes down to the individuals and teams.

Team Examples

This is the American political model (at least in the ideal) of states supporting a federal government and the federal level strengthening the states. A similar pattern is followed in many states as they work with the counties. Likewise, in Canada, the provinces accomplish the same things with the national government. The Swiss cantons apply a similar model in relation to the nation.

Indeed, the federal or national government is stronger with more states or provinces, and if it is effectively limited to its proper role, a stronger national-level government is a better support to the states.

This same model can be applied in many settings. For example, a national sports league is typically stronger and better at accomplishing its goals with thirty-two teams than with twenty-eight (e.g., the National Football League). The same holds true with hockey, basketball, baseball, soccer, etc. And the better the individual teams, the better it is for the league as a whole.

It is possible, Toffler argues, for both popular views to be true: bigger is better, and small is beautiful.[44] This only works, however, if all levels stick to their appropriate roles. The key word is *appropriate*.[45] The most important units are the individual, the team, the group, the cohort, the multitudes, and the leadership of the whole. Each is vital. And when rightly structured, each greatly strengthens and benefits the others.

Leaders build organizations that flourish at the small level and also at the large level. This is especially true in the Networking Economy of the twenty-first century.

The Guide

This brings us to a fifth key of engaging entrepreneurial success in the new economy: mentoring. The twenty-first-century replacement for the expert is the wise, broad-minded mentor. The best mentors are simply those who have achieved the things you want to achieve.

The era of the expert is over, or at least in decline. Toffler wrote: "Today, in every field, including politics, we see a basic change in attitude toward the expert. Once regarded as the trustworthy source of neutral intelligence, specialists have been dethroned from public approval. They are increasingly criticized for pursuing their own self-interest and for being incapable of anything but tunnel vision."[46]

The era of the mentor is in. Find a mentor who has learned how to thrive doing what you want to accomplish, and learn from him or her. Such a mentor does not need badges of honor, credentials from certified sources, or other trappings that the "expert" covets. Good mentors need merely that rarest of proofs of their suitability, namely, fruit on the tree.

Such experience is exactly what you need to get on the right path, in the right way, and work toward your goals. In the previous chapter, we noted that in the twenty-first-century marketplace, mentors are the new "college." As important as this is, your business/life purpose mentor is even *more* vital.

Leaders will greatly benefit from reading perhaps the most important book on mentors, entitled *Mentoring Matters*, which is part of the Life Leadership Essentials Series. It is available at lifeleadership.com. Since mentoring is becoming incredibly important in the new economy, this excellent book is a must for professionals, business leaders, young people considering college decisions (and their parents), and anyone who will benefit from the right kind of mentoring.

Whatever way you choose to pursue a great college-level and even graduate-level education, when you are ready to embrace your career focus, getting and following the guidance of an effective and proven mentor is downright essential. It will make or break you, in most cases.

Again, for most people in the new economy, building a successful business is the new career. And the mentor you choose to work with will largely determine how well you do.

PARADIGM
5

Principles Are the New Political Parties

We set up a system whereby the [political officials] only made money when their [citizens] made money. We overlapped the needs and the goals of the [political officials] with the needs and goals of the...people.
—STEPHEN COVEY [QUOTE MODIFIED FROM BUSINESS TO POLITICS][47]

It is impossible for us to break the [moral] law. We can only break ourselves against the law.
—CECIL B. DEMILLE

In his magnum opus, *Democracy in America*, Alexis de Tocqueville noted that every free nation breaks into two great political parties: the party of aristocracy and the party of democracy. (Authoritarian nations tend to split between the party of the king, or dictator, and the party of aristocracy, or oligarchy.)

In England and its early American colonies, including those in Canada, the eighteenth century was characterized by ongoing skirmishes between the Whigs (democracy) and the Tories (aristocracy). After the American Revolution, the Federalists and Anti-Federalists confused the issue a bit because the Anti-Federalists favored increased democracy at the national level and simultaneously held on to the traditions of aristocracy within the states and locales, and the Federalists generally preferred the opposite.

After the US Constitution was ratified, the Federalists maintained their stance, and the new Democratic-Republican Party adopted something very close to the former Anti-Federalist view.

All of this can be frustrating for a student of history to remember, but it was even more frustrating for the citizens of the time to endure. And it mirrored the struggles of political parties in history.

The Party Problem

As David Hume wrote, for example: "Men have such a propensity to divide into [political parties],[48] that the smallest appearance of real difference will produce them. What can be imagined more trivial than the difference between one colour of livery [saddle and bridle] and another in horse races? Yet this difference begat two most [inflexible political parties] in the Greek Empire...who never suspended their animosities till they ruined that unhappy government."[49]

Hume also noted that political parties "subvert government, render laws impotent, and beget the fiercest animosities among men of the same nation, who ought to give mutual assistance and protection of each other…and… they always infect the legislature itself."[50]

Many of the American founders quoted Hume on this topic, and many of them warned against the dangers of political parties. In *Federalist Papers* 10 and 14, for example, James Madison predicted that the agendas of political parties and the subsequent partisanship of the citizens could be the biggest danger to the newly formed nation.

This was a big enough problem that Madison and Alexander Hamilton addressed it in *Federalist Papers* 8, 9, 15, 16, 18, 21, 22, 27, 29, 51, 59, 61, 65, 70, 71, 73, and 81. Clearly they were concerned with the potential negatives of political parties.

> **James Madison predicted that the agendas of political parties and the subsequent partisanship of the citizens could be the biggest danger to the newly formed United States.**

The Original Solution

In fact, the Framers of the US Constitution specifically tried to avoid letting political parties obtain power in the United States by setting up a voting arrangement where the person receiving the most votes for president would be elected, and the person receiving the second most votes would be the vice-president. The idea was that this combination of electing the top two candidates wouldn't allow a political party system to get a foothold in the federal government.

Since the two top candidates would likely be from different parties, the founders reasoned, this would require them to work together more often — lessening the power of any one party.

It was a good model and worked as planned from 1789 until the heated disagreements between the Federalists and Democratic-Republicans dominated the election of 1800. Before that, elections under this system were full of passion and intensity, but political parties didn't overtake the whole operation of government.

If fact, it was the desires of zealous Federalists and also Democratic-Republicans to have more power for their respective parties that drove support for more partisanship in the 1800 election. This same focus created momentum for the Twelfth Amendment, which changed the original constitutional mode of electing the president and vice-president and put them on the same ticket representing one party.

Parties always strive to increase their influence, and after the Twelfth Amendment passed in 1804, the political party system in America grew rapidly, soon becoming a shadow government in every city, state, small town, and neighborhood — exactly what the Framers had tried to avoid.

> **Parties always strive to increase their influence.**

Thomas Jefferson tried to take a step back from the party system after this election. He told the American people in his inaugural address: "We have called by different names brethren of the same principle. We are all Republicans—we are all Federalists."[51]

But the damage had already been done, and with a foothold in presidential elections, the spirit of party spread throughout the political landscape. Jefferson defended his partisanship during the election by arguing that the opposing Federalist agenda was too strong and too wrong and needed to be stopped.

In later years, he lamented this move to party politics and felt that it had been a bad choice for the nation. Likewise in his later years, John Adams, who had opposed Jefferson from the Federalist side of the partisan conflict, agreed that the slide to party politics had done more harm than good.

Fast Forward...

Today, the spread of political parties is almost complete. The parties dominate almost the entire political system in the United States, including even what the Framers wanted to be entirely nonpartisan deliberations and decisions of the Supreme Court. Almost nothing now occurs in North American politics—town, city, state, province, or national level—without the influence of the top parties.

> Almost nothing now occurs in North American politics—town, city, state, province, or national level—without the influence of the top parties.

This is true in elections, certainly, but also in the day-to-day operations of government. Party influence is hugely impactful even on nonelected government employees working in agencies and bureaucracies at all levels.

Other nations have experienced similar negatives from the undue power of parties. The victory of political parties is complete in the West. When the leading parties agree, they are a juggernaut of power—from Washington to Berlin and from London to Ottawa to Paris and beyond.

When they disagree, their debates, antics, and struggles dominate the news—sometimes (frequently, in fact, in the age of dedicated political TV channels) holding a nation hostage in breathless anticipation of outcomes on an important issue and then repeating the drama a week or month later.

Yet this level of partisan success has set the stage for its own demise, in a way. In the United States, for example, in recent years, more citizens see themselves as independents than as either Democrats or Republicans. This doesn't materially change the vote for president, but it significantly influences everything else about American politics.

A Second Trend

In addition to this rise of self-described independents to majority status (a quiet but major revolution), another factor is bringing massive change: the new and sweeping universality of the Internet. Together these two shifts have drastically changed the partisan playing field.

On the one hand, both top US political parties court independents and use the Internet to spread their message to multiple target audiences and voting demographics. This has created a new, sophisticated politicization of many groups—driven by big money working in concert with one of the major parties.

On the other hand, the leveling power of the Internet has actually decreased party influence for a large segment of citizens. They get their political news elsewhere, mainly from friends, thought leaders, and people they trust—as discussed in the earlier chapter on media.

The question is which of these two trends will win out. Will the political parties dominate the Internet—at least on the topic of politics—as they did the television airwaves in the TV era? Or will personal political views exert more influence?

A New Democratic Age

So far the contest isn't even close. Personal views dwarf the influence of official parties in the virtual world. Indeed, the Internet has the most anti-partisan sway of any major modern communication technology—more than the telephone, radio, television, or movies.

David Brooks of *The New York Times* has pointed out that few Internet users spend much time objectively studying both sides of deep political issues. They typically just frequent the websites and sources they like and ignore opposing viewpoints. But they also engage political and cultural topics by listening to regular people, peers and friends, normal citizens, much more than in past decades.

This is creating a democratizing effect, where more and more people are engaging important political conversations with other regular people in casual settings where political parties hold very little sway — a serious and potentially profound change from the past. Coming as this does within a decade or two of a widespread national loss of trust in experts, it has the makings of a major transformation in America.

> **More and more people are engaging important political conversations with other regular people in casual settings where political parties hold very little sway.**

Likewise, since 9/11, another trend has gained increased support — a deepening loss of trust in major institutions. Partisanship has influenced this change. For example, more conservatives tend to mistrust the FBI or Ivy League university professors, while more liberals mistrust the CIA or Wall Street. But most major public institutions have drastically decreased in popularity across the board.

People now tend to put more trust in other ordinary people and listen more carefully to their ideas than they did during the postwar era — while institutions have a strike against them before they even start trying to influence society. Whatever the institutions say, many people are inclined to be skeptical.

Next Turn...

If these trends hold, or even gain momentum, the next step is likely a long overdue turn to principles above parties.

Unlike the first four paradigm shifts discussed in earlier chapters, the move from parties to principles may not fully bloom. The others are all but assured. But this one could still go either way, depending on what happens in the years just ahead.

> People now tend to put more trust in other ordinary people and listen more carefully to their ideas than they did during the postwar era.

That said, if we do continue the current shift to principles as the new technologically empowered focus of our politics (and all indications are that this is the most likely outcome), the major question arises: Just what, exactly, will this look like? After all, political parties are so dominant in modern free nations that it's hard for most people to concretely picture a governmental system where principles rule instead of parties.

> Political parties are so dominant in modern free nations that it's hard for most people to concretely picture a governmental system where principles rule instead of parties.

A New Tapestry

Actually, much of the groundwork has already been laid by the "principle-centered" revolution that occurred in business during the last quarter of the twentieth century. Stephen Covey described this phenomenon as three distinct eras in leadership and the corresponding management literature.

Period #1: Great Leadership

Before the mid-twentieth century, what Covey called the "Character Ethic" dominated. Quality, excellence, integrity, and principles were the central focus of leadership—and of training leaders. In this period, books and materials on leadership weren't seen as a separate genre. Some rose to the status of classics, others were bestsellers, and many were simply books—not relegated to the business section but on the main library shelf.

Indeed, one of the first great leadership books was Plutarch's *Parallel Lives*, which compared various leaders of Greek and Roman history and outlined their effective versus not-so-effective leadership traits and decisions.[52] Other classics that dealt extensively with leadership include *Meditations* by Marcus Aurelius, *Confessions* by St. Augustine, *Don Quixote* by Cervantes, *War and Peace* by Tolstoy, *Les Misérables* by Hugo, and, of course, the Bible. (Just consider, for example, the leadership messages of Exodus 18:13–26, Deuteronomy 1:9–17, and the four gospels in the New Testament.) Other great leadership works in the pre-twentieth-century era included Dante's *Divine Comedy*, Swift's *Gulliver's Travels*, and Gibbon's *Decline and Fall of the Roman Empire*. The writings of Shakespeare, Austen, Benjamin Franklin, and others also dealt substantially with such themes.

The leadership messages of such works most often emphasized values such as duty, virtue, honor, service, compassion, judgment, and wisdom.

Period #2: The Personality Era

But during the twentieth century, Covey taught, something changed. The early focus on moral leadership, the "Character Ethic," was replaced by a new focus on the "Personality Ethic."[53] "Change your personality and upgrade your techniques and skills, and you'll find success," the new view promised.[54]

Covey wrote:

> The Character Ethic taught that there are basic principles of effective living, and that people can only experience true success and enduring happiness as they learn and integrate these principles into their basic character.
>
> But shortly after World War I the basic view of success shifted from the Character Ethic to what we might call the *Personality Ethic*. Success became more a function of personality, of public image, of attitudes and behaviors, skills and techniques, that lubricate the processes of human interaction. This Personality

Ethic essentially took two paths: one was human and public relations techniques, and the other was positive mental attitude (PMA).[55]

Out of this grew the self-help and business management genres, which revolutionized publishing around the same time that Whyte wrote *The Organization Man*. This formed a foundation for the management industry of the 1950s through the 1990s and hugely influenced business, education, and society.

Period #3: A Return to Character

Later thought leaders like Covey, Peter Drucker, and Buckminster Fuller noted the need for a return to the Character Ethic, and this alteration, though it developed slowly, began to influence business through the 1990s and into the twenty-first century. The new emphasis of leadership literature during this shift is on increased "integrity, maturity, genuineness, and abundance mentality."[56]

Skills and techniques are still important, of course, but the focus is on the true purpose of leadership—and each leader's true life purpose.

But how can this change in business translate to the political realm? This is a crucial question.

Influence Beyond Business

The answer is interesting. Major cultural changes in business and the marketplace usually occur a few decades before governments adopt them, and this happens a decade or more before most educational institutions join in. Thus, today we are currently on track for such a shift in politics and governance.

No legal or constitutional changes need to be made in the United States or in most free nations to effect this paradigm shift. Voters with a different mindset — not trusting in parties or dependent on party leaders but simply studying the issues and candidates and voting according to principle — have all the power to bring this about. Some are already doing so.

As more voters follow suit, the paradigm shift will naturally occur. Legal changes may result (e.g., altering the direct role of parties in Congressional procedures), but even if they don't, a new way of voting will bring about significant improvements. The voters have the power in this regard.

The overall goal is to change the negative synergy of warring political parties and partisans to the positive synergy of nonpartisan voters who simply care about the future of our nation, communities, families, businesses, and people.

> **Major cultural changes in business and the marketplace usually occur a few decades before governments adopt them, and this happens a decade or more before most educational institutions join in.**

> **The overall goal is to change the negative synergy of warring political parties.**

What to Do

The first step to becoming such a voter is to start studying elections more closely—before the vote. Study what the major issues are in the election and what the candidates stand for. Study what both sides say about the issues, and then go deeper: find out what nonpartisan sources say as well. Really know what your vote is about, who the candidates truly are, and what your vote will mean to the future.

Such self-informed voters are the real power in any free nation. As they grow in numbers, the people are increasingly truly free. The Internet has made this kind of voter independence much easier than at any point in history, but voters will only wield such power if they individually seek and utilize it. Freedom is in our hands at a rate never even dreamed of by generations past.

The question for us is simple: Will we use this power, or will we ignore this opportunity and leave politics to the professionals and a small activist/elite class of voters? If we choose the latter, the political party system will continue to flourish. If we choose the former, however, citizenship will eclipse partisanship—and freedom and prosperity will naturally benefit.

Again, this paradigm shift could still go either way. We get to decide. If we as modern free citizens exert the powers that are now available to us before, during, and after elections, we can put the undue power of political parties behind us and govern by principle.

It's our choice.

A Growing Consensus

In all this, there is a growing collection of shared ideas that are garnering more and more supporters. When regular people leave party labels out of their conversations, it's often amazing how much they agree on what is needed in our society. Of course, there are certainly still some disagreements. But without the baggage of partisanship, positive conversations and realistic, sound solutions are more abundant.

> When regular people leave party labels out of their conversations, it's often amazing how much they agree on what is needed in our society.

For example, there are a lot of hardworking middle-class Americans who share a core set of values. And, surprisingly for many who consider partisanship and the conservative/liberal debate the central American theme, people with these shared values make up the majority in both red and blue states and both parties. They are also the majority of independents. Again, take political parties and labels out of the dialogue, and we have more in common than in dispute.

> Take political parties and labels out of the dialogue, and we have more in common than in dispute.

We can no longer just vote on a candidate or two and call it good, not if we want to reverse the current decline and build the kind of nations we can be truly proud of. We have to go a few steps further, to envision what we really want, share it with others, learn from them, and create a national vision.

> We can no longer just vote on a candidate or two and call it good, not if we want to reverse the current decline and build the kind of nations we can be truly proud of.

To join the current "Great Conversation," to borrow a phrase from Mortimer Adler, we need to start thinking and communicating about the type of nation and society we want to build in our lifetimes. Otherwise, we leave such planning to governments and corporations. That's the old model, not the new — the partisan approach, not the principled path.

The Battle

To understand what's really at stake, it helps to consider what the elite, big government/big business, partisan-based approach actually is right now.

For example, what is the culture of our current elite class? The answer is interesting and enlightening. As David Brooks outlined in a study of today's elites,[57] their code of behavior is different from that of most Americans. The US power elite class (and this holds true for most of their counterparts in other free nations) tends to emphasize:

- Prestigious degrees (with a habit of both mentioning but also understating such credentials)

- Making lots of money, mostly in corporate jobs with large expense accounts and liberal benefit packages (and understating their compensation in a "code of financial correctness")[58]
- Buying mostly necessities, not a lot of luxuries[59]
- Generally only buying top "professional quality" goods and services in everything[60]
- Practicing "the perfectionism of small things" in all walks of life[61]
- Practicing "one-downmanship" by adorning their lives with the casual and "peasanty" — in other words, expensive simplicity that sets them apart from the middle class striving to surround itself with various trappings of wealth[62]
- When in doubt, says the elite code, invoke *Walden*.[63]

Shakespeare and Sartre — or even better, Thomas Piketty — are always in vogue with the elite class as well.[64] The elite mode is to avoid any appearance of a consumerist, "impress others at all costs" culture such as those modeled in various reality TV programs, including the *Real Housewives of...Anywhere*.

The Shadows

There is, however, a darker side to this seemingly softer, gentler elitism. Under the surface, the battles for power are more competitive than ever. Let's see how this plays out in two important ways.

First, a dominant idea within the modern elite class is to regulate oneself "with health codes instead of moral codes."[65] For example, Brooks describes modern, urban, elite society as a place where almost any kind of sexual choice is accepted but where people "are outraged if they see a pregnant woman smoking."[66] Health codes trump morality in the elite world.

Second, and just as disturbing to many mainstream American sensibilities, many in the elite class maintain a smug arrogance, a belief in their "real superiority," as Mr. Darcy might put it.[67] A 2015 article in *The Atlantic* captured this in a single powerful snapshot. Reporting about elite investment bankers during the period leading up to the economy's collapse of 2008 and the beginning of the Great Recession, William D. Cohan wrote: "A common attitude...was 'It is not enough to succeed. Others must fail.'"[68]

> The idea that "others must fail," presented in an attitude of "us versus them" and "we're better than them," flies in the face of mid-America's most cherished beliefs about society, life, work, fairness, opportunity, freedom, and how the economy should function.

Similarly, after researching what works most often in elite business organizations, Wharton professor Adam Grant said: "What I've become convinced of is that nice guys and gals really do finish last."[69]

This picture doesn't sit well with most Americans. It is, in fact, a direct challenge to middle-American values. Grant went on to show that "takers" don't get ahead as often as "givers" in elite culture but that "disagreeable givers" often do get ahead more than others.[70] He also clarifies that "giving" and "being nice" aren't the same thing.[71]

But the idea that "others must fail," presented in an attitude of "us versus them" and "we're better than them," flies in the face of mid-America's most cherished beliefs about society, life, work, fairness, opportunity, freedom, and how the economy should function.

If this haughty attitude (carefully hidden by PR professionals) is new to you, welcome to the battle for the future of our culture. The good news is that there are a lot more mid-American voters than elite voters. The bad news is that elites generally pay better attention to politics and make their influence felt more often than the masses. In fact, the top political parties and their ongoing clashes are both run mostly by elites.

> **The bad news is that elites generally pay better attention to politics and make their influence felt more often than the masses.**

But that can change. Voters can transform this system to one where principles rule. Or we can sit back, the way many voters have in past decades,

> **Voters can transform the current system to one where principles rule.**

and simply let the elites and political partisans run the show. We get to choose. And in the era of the Internet, our power is right at our fingertips—easier to wield and more effective than ever before in history.

It's up to us.

But that's the good news, if we want it to be. Repeat that phrase again: It's up to us.

It really is.

Megashifts

In short, a new power to promote principles is available to us right now. As John Naisbitt wrote in his bestselling book *Megatrends*: "People whose lives are affected by a decision must be part of the process of arriving at that decision."[72] Therefore, in his words, we need a shift to more "participatory democracy"[73] where "the new leader is a facilitator, not an order giver."[74]

Naisbitt's words also provide one of the most significant evidences that we may now be on the verge of a paradigm shift from parties to principles: "Change occurs when there is a confluence of both changing values and economic necessity, not before."[75] Today many anti-partisan value changes have already occurred, and more and more people realize that political decisions are directly relevant to our bank accounts.

This goes along with Naisbitt's additional forecast that we are moving as a society from "Institutional-Help to Self-Help."[76] This has already revolutionized and restructured our media, educational, and business sectors, and government is naturally the next domino.

Whether this is enough to bring solid principles of freedom and prosperity — rather than political parties — to the forefront in our nation is up to the voters.

We will decide.

The challenge to each of us is to decide wisely.

PARADIGM
6

Wellness Is the New Health Care

In the new self-help paradigm, prevention is clearly more sensible and cheaper than cure.

—JOHN NAISBITT

Any patient in a hospital, when we take their clothes away and lay them in a bed, starts to lose identity.

—TERRENCE HOLT

Let's just get straight to the point about our sixth great paradigm shift. Here goes:

Old Reality	New Reality
Pharmacies	Vegetables
Doctors	Fruit
Specialists	Exercise
Surgeries	Sunshine
Casts	Rest

Old Reality	New Reality
Pills	Nutrition
Stitches	Fresh Air
Insurance	Water
Shots	Prevention
Band-Aids	Work
Painkillers	Health
Nurses	Smiling
Emergency Rooms	Friends
Hospitals	Service
Doctor Bills	Purpose
Waiting Rooms	Life
Diagnoses	Vitality
Needles	Fitness

Enough said.

Got it? Okay, let's move on to the next chapter.

***

Just kidding. Actually, if we did share only this list, it would be a significant approach to the topic. The shift to focusing on personal wellness is a major change in our modern society.

But let's say a little bit more about it.

Challenges

First of all, modern life is often very stressful. Not that human life hasn't always carried its share of difficulties. It has. But even though in modern times we usually don't have to worry about lions or barbarians waiting for us just outside our caves or huts, we still have our share of concerns.

Besides, our bodies are designed to relieve the stress caused by lions and barbarians. As we fight them or flee from them, we release the hormones our bodies pump into our bloodstreams for just such occasions. But in the modern world—no such luck. We still get pumped full of adrenaline, cortisol, and other fight-or-flight chemicals, but they don't usually get released right away.

> **Even though in modern times we usually don't have to worry about lions or barbarians waiting for us just outside our caves or huts, we still have our share of concerns.**

And the food we eat, and the way we eat it (on the run, late at night, in a hurry before the next meeting, as we drive, etc.) adds even more toxins our bodies have to process. Not good.

Not to mention how many moderns fall into sedentary habits. We sit—a lot. And most people don't exercise enough. We know we should, but…things get in the way. So many things. So busy. So much to do.

But enough on that topic. We all know we should exercise more, drink more water (and less of other beverages), get enough sleep, go to bed earlier, eat less, eat better, eat a lot more vegetables, and on and on. We know this stuff.

The Divide

What we might not realize, unless we really think about it, is that a division now exists between two groups of people: those who are basically healthy and those who are increasingly unhealthy. For decades, the general cultural view has been that it's okay to be a bit unhealthy—that's what doctors are for. If you get really sick, the health-care industry will be there to make everything better. Right?

> For decades, the general cultural view has been that it's okay to be a bit unhealthy—that's what doctors are for.

But this idea is changing, and, in fact, it never was a very sound viewpoint. With socialized medicine in most "free" nations, really top-rate health care is harder to find and a lot more expensive when you do get it. Besides that, the view that some expert will fix me if I lose my health due to bad lifestyle choices is downright wrongheaded.

A lot of people held that perspective over the past fifty years, yes. Some still do. But it's simply false—and dangerous. If you don't have your health, your standard of life will drastically decrease. Period.

Fortunately, as faith in experts and institutions dwindles, more people are taking active responsibility for their own health. Thankfully, we still have medical professionals and surgeons for legitimate emergencies, but more people today are taking the initiative to engage the day-to-day actions that bring more health, vibrancy, and energy.

If you are part of this second group, good. If not, if you're on the wrong side of the self-health divide, it's time to take action. It's time to get healthy by simply making healthier choices.

The World Ahead

When Royal Dutch Shell commissioned a large group of leaders from a number of fields to come together, research, and forecast what to expect in the world in the years leading up to 2025 and beyond, the team surprised a lot of people with its predictions. They're worth considering, especially if you are a leader or will be a leader in the years ahead.

First, the researchers discovered, the decades ahead are likely to be dominated by several important perspectives held by citizens around the world—in highly advanced nations as well as those still struggling for better economic opportunities and improved lifestyles. These include:[77]

- Low levels of trust
- High levels of fear
- A strong need for security

These challenges were almost universal for all nations. In fact, they form a kind of Emotional State of the World for the decades ahead. Sad, when you think about it.

Second, what differed between nations, geographic regions, and socioeconomic groups in the report was the various potential responses to these concerns. Some nations and groups are likely to address them with more government programs and regulations, others with more support from local governments, and still others with more programs from international organizations—both governmental and private.[78]

Two additional options stood out: 1) solutions from more effective and aggressive voluntary and private communities and affiliate organizations, and 2) improved results brought on by increased market incentives[79] (meaning, mainly, reduced government regulations and increased entrepreneurialism).

But whatever happens with governments, corporations, communities, and voluntary organizations, the initial reality should concern every modern leader: We live in a world where fear is high and likely growing, where trust in institutions or getting help from other people is low, and where people worry about the basic safety and security of their families. This is all compounded by a predominantly sedentary lifestyle and a less-than-ideal nutritional environment.

> **We live in a world where fear is high and likely growing, where trust in institutions or getting help from other people is low, and where people worry about the basic safety and security of their families.**

Health will be a growing concern in the next fifty years, just as it has been for the last fifty. But right now, we're starting from a place of vulnerability and lower health than before.

Health is of paramount importance. And, as the experts warn, governments simply aren't going to be able to meet the demands. Many would argue that this isn't government's role anyway.

So whose role is it? And how can they carry it out?

The Self-Health Revolution

Put bluntly, barring major catastrophe—like an earthquake or the use of weapons of mass destruction—your health is up to you. This is true for every individual and family. But as mentioned above, not everyone understands this.

Thus the first step is to take responsibility for your own health—to lead out. The second is to help others learn to do the same. It is especially important to teach this to your own family and in your community.

> **Put bluntly, barring major catastrophe—like an earthquake or the use of weapons of mass destruction—your health is up to you.**

A third step is to know enough about the topics of health care, medical care, and self-health (with a focus on wellness) to be able to converse wisely about these things with others—not just about good health practices, like eating well and getting consistent exercise, but also about the public policy aspect of health care and self-health.

In the years ahead, governments will increasingly try to regulate this field. This raises the stakes for voters (to vote wisely) and for individuals and families (to actively improve self-health practices that emphasize wellness).

It is to this third point that we now turn our attention.

Where We Are

Perhaps nowhere did more people put as much trust in experts from the 1950s through the 1980s as in the field of health care. As we mentioned before, Alvin Toffler referred to medical doctors in this era as veritable "gods in white coats." When doctors gave their decrees, people were expected to listen and obey. And most did.

Like a number of other things, this began to change in a serious way with the advent of the Internet. The ability to research medical conditions, treatments, and commentaries online threw a wrench into the power of doctors.

Before the Internet, most patients received one medical opinion or sometimes two. But the Internet put a dozen or more medical opinions at the patient's fingertips, as well as studies, opposing studies, rebuttals to each recommended line of treatment, and doctors arguing with doctors.

The cloak of infallibility that many people attributed to doctors, and even more so to "specialists," couldn't stand up in the face of so many different, often divergent viewpoints from the doctors themselves. It quickly became clear to any newly-diagnosed patient who bothered to research his or her condition online that doctors were doing something startling: they were *practicing* medicine.

Practice on Somebody Else, Please

Practicing means experimenting, learning how to treat patients by observing what works and what doesn't, trying to apply the best procedures, treatments, and techniques based on the experience of other doctors as well, and going with the averages—and then repeating the whole experiment when new information comes along. The medical profession has never denied this approach. To the contrary, it has been very open about it.

But it took the Internet for a majority of patients to finally get the message. The linchpin in this shift came with social media. Now patients could read the experiences of a dozen other people with the same prognosis. What worked? What went wrong? What was hard? What mistakes were made? What diagnoses were flawed—and what was the final and more accurate diagnosis?

Also, what treatments or approaches were effective? Which weren't? What were the side effects, if any? What else happened? What would patients do differently if they had to do it all again? What should be avoided? What should be done right away?

> Patients no longer waited for the doctor's word on every detail and trusted it without question. As a result, a newly empowered era of self-help erupted.

Increased Empowerment

These and other questions put a lot more decision-making power into the hands of patients, who no longer waited for the doctor's word on every detail and trusted it without question. As a result, a newly empowered era of self-help erupted.

"I think our best course of action is to try a round of antibiotics first and then see..."

"Sorry to interrupt you, Doctor Smith, but I just read an article in the *New England Journal of Medicine* that says a new study shows that it would be better to..."

Many doctors began paying closer attention to the latest journals, and others simply kept more specialists' phone numbers on hand. Some patients stuck with the old path of just following the doctor, but a lot of them started shopping around, researching, comparing and contrasting, and above all, talking at length with each other online — questioning every medical decision.

Rating systems that grade doctors (along with dentists, hospitals, etc.) in every specialty in town appeared, with long comment sections from former and current patients. Such bottom-up discussions invariably addressed the various ways people could improve their situation through lifestyle or other choices.

The result, as mentioned, was an explosion of self-care. Yes, emergency medicine and surgery maintained some of the aura of the old White Coat era. After all, YouTube tutorials on brain surgery are hard to come by, and they wouldn't exactly meet a standard most patients are comfortable with anyway. And when you need medical help after a serious emergency, surfing the Internet isn't your first thought in most cases.

So not all medicine turned to the self-health arena. But a staggering proportion of what had once been considered the sole purview of doctors now became the focus of individuals and families. Perhaps most important, common sense rejoined the dialogue, and more people took more responsibility for their actions concerning their health.

> A staggering proportion of what had once been considered the sole purview of doctors now became the focus of individuals and families.

Many people changed their view of the lifestyle diseases from health concerns requiring pharmaceuticals and surgeries to problems demanding better nutrition, stress reduction, and consistent exercise. And a number of formerly accepted habits—from smoking to high sugar intake—became mainstream family concerns.

In all this, the emphasis shifted from after-the-fact responses to illness to a more preventive, before-the-fact emphasis on wellness. If we live a healthier lifestyle, people realized, we'll be well rather than sick—at least more so than if we don't take care of ourselves.

The Vegetable Revolution

In a way, vegetables were the winners in this transition. People worried that they weren't eating enough vegetables, that their children weren't eating enough vegetables, and that their elderly parents weren't eating enough vegetables. Some people took this so far that they worried about the people in their neighborhood or church group eating enough vegetables.

The Vegetable Revolution influenced school lunches, initiatives from the White House, the legal size of soda drinks in some cities, and the makeup of the healthy daily portions chart taught in high school health courses. In entertainment, the cartoon character Popeye and his love of spinach didn't make the national comeback that some vegetable lovers had hoped, but a generation of children did go around singing numerous songs about "VeggieTales."

Among those motivated by the Vegetable Revolution, numerous debates arose between factions—some promoting organic foods only, some decrying GMOs, some arguing that modern vegetables lack nutrients and supplementing them with various brands of powders and capsules, others recommending various pills and health drinks and supplements, some replacing all meats with extra servings of veggies, some leaving the meat but getting rid of all processed foods (anything packaged in boxes, bags, or cans), and still others making the case that only raw, fresh fruits and vegetables are really healthy foods for the body.

Many of these trends helped people pay more attention to and improve their own health. Not every product thrived, and not every family ate all their vegetables. But a number of people improved their health awareness and, in many cases, their health practices.

Thousands of books came out on these and other health-related topics over the decades, and numerous seminars, workshops, and conferences made the rounds across North America. Home gardening and greenhousing experienced a major resurgence, as some people wanted to take quality nutrition to an even higher level. Farmers' markets proliferated in both cities and small towns.

> **Home gardening and greenhousing experienced a major resurgence, as some people wanted to take quality nutrition to an even higher level.**

Far from being a mere fad, this shift had a real impact on the eating habits of many households. As mentioned, a lot of people ate more vegetables and a lot more healthy foods. The Vegetable Revolution never caught on as the mainstream American way of eating, and it didn't end the popularity of sweet, fried, or fast foods. But it did influence a significant number of people to eat better in general.

> **One of the great enemies of the American health "revolution" turned out to be the television.**

A Couch Potato?

One of the great enemies of the American health "revolution" turned out to be the television. If this were a comic book or graphic novel, the conflict might be portrayed as the Vegetable Revolution versus the Couch Potato. Ominous, right?

And make no mistake: this is a "take-no-prisoners" battle. Your health choices ensure that you ultimately belong to either one side or the other.

For example, one study showed that "for every two hours of TV you watch a day, you're 23 percent more likely to become obese (and 14 percent more likely to develop diabetes)."[80] In fact, more than two-thirds of Americans are now overweight.[81] These are big numbers.

But the research shows that this is just the beginning of the problem. Consistent hours of sitting in front of the TV often create an abnormal curvature of the spine[82] and can shrink lung capacity by approximately a third.[83] Not good.

"An Australian study of national health records found that, on average, every single hour of TV watching after age 25 reduces life expectancy by close to 22 minutes."[84] Other researchers found that "people who say they watch TV 'very often' are 40 percent more likely than non-TV watchers to exercise less than one hour a week."[85] Only one hour a week? That's bad.

It all adds up to one thing: watch less TV or none at all. Coach soccer instead, or just play basketball with your kids. Or plant and grow a garden. Or start and build a business. "Get off the couch, and get a life," as the last two generations of Americans have been saying to themselves.

But don't just talk to yourself about this. Actually do it. The health benefits are huge.

Researchers found that, on average, people who watch TV before bed get less sleep and wake up less rested than those who skip it because the "'blue light' TVs emit inhibits the release of melatonin, a hormone that helps you" sleep.[86]

By the way, these research studies all dealt with adults. The long-term problems for kids who watch too many hours of TV are even worse.

Take Charge

Beyond eating more vegetables, reducing junk food intake, and cutting down our time in front of the TV, the self-health revolution is based on a few more key suggestions. Each is really just a return to common sense in how we treat our bodies.

In the book *Should I Fire My Doctor?*, for example, Patricia J. Sulak, MD, recommends the following:

- Move your body at least an hour every day.[87]
- "Halt harmful habits."[88]
- "Forgive: family, friends, foes, and [yourself]."[89]
- Serve people.[90]
- Find your life purpose, and pursue it with passion.[91]
- Overcome stress.[92]
- Take time to "periodically pause, ponder, plan, and pray."[93]

> It's surprising, in fact, that in modern society we ever stopped caring about health.

All of these are powerful and effective tools of self-health. Each one emphasizes wellness, not just waiting until your health declines to take positive action. It's surprising, in fact, that in modern society we ever stopped caring about health.

The Old Days and Middle

But let's go a bit deeper. To do this, let's take a few moments, back up, and trace the history of health care in the twentieth century and into the twenty-first. All of us need to know about this important part of modern life.

The first major period of modern health care is the time before World War II and could be called the era of the family doctor. In this period, many a doctor did house calls, knew the families he (or sometimes she) served over the course of long years of interaction—often from birth through parenthood—and served as a wise counselor and even comfort to families in times of illness, emergency, tragedy, and death.

The family doctor was a friend, in many cases, and at the very least a staple in the community.

Then, during the overall cultural "Organization Man" era from 1945 to around 2005, the doctor took on a different role. Actually, doctors and lawyers filled a niche more aptly described as "The Professional Man" during this time period. Professional Men differed from Organization Men in several important ways.

Professionals were seen as the experts, for example. In many cases, a town doctor (or a specific family doctor in the cities and suburbs) was the only expert a family consulted on health issues. Thus the doctor was both an expert and a generalist expected to know a lot about everything related to health. People listened with believing ears to almost everything the doctor told them.

During this era, however, specialists also proliferated. The corporate model that dominated society significantly influenced the medical profession, creating vast hierarchies and complex health institution flow charts with boxes, arrows, appendices, and footnotes. Doctors, nurses, practitioners, surgeons, and a host of other specialties each played various roles in the overall machine.

The Impersonal Era

If patients weren't always sure how it all worked, somebody was at least there to tell them whom to talk to next— at which address and on what specific date and time.

The system frequently operated in mechanical (rather than organic) terms. In other words, the process of finding and rooting out disease was the focus of the health-care industry and its practitioners. The concerns, convenience, ease, and worries of patients were not the priority.

> The process of finding and rooting out disease was the focus of the health-care industry and its practitioners.

Experts ruled from the top, staffers put their words into action with an often-chaotic professional efficiency, and patients were expected to follow orders. This frequently looked like the schools for youth and the convalescent homes for the elderly in the same era—where experts assessed and issued orders while workers tried to be efficient.

Thus many students in schools, many elderly in convalescent homes, and many patients in hospitals were often seen by the professionals as passive recipients. Active participation by these recipients was frequently viewed as tantamount to rebellion—or at least a time-consuming distraction.

As one report described the situation: "Spend a day in an emergency room, and chances are you'll be struck by...the organizational chaos and the emotional detachment as nurses, doctors, and administrators bustle in and out, barely registering the human distress it is their job to address."[94]

This sense of robot-like health care is sad on the medical level as well as for humane concerns. For example, as Danielle Ofri, MD, an expert on the medical profession (and an internist at Bellevue Hospital in New York) noted: "The rate of severe diabetes complications in patients of doctors who rate high on a standard empathy scale...is a remarkable 40 percent lower than in patients with low-empathy doctors."[95] Ofri offers a number of similar examples in her book *What Doctors Feel*.

Some doctors, many nurses, and other health-care professionals during this period made it their additional purpose to really connect with colleagues, patients, and the loved ones of patients on a deeper, comforting, and compassionate human level. Others were known for their aloof bedside manner.

Hurry Up and Wait

A distinct feature of this era was the long waits most patients faced each time they had an appointment with their doctor or specialist.

Whereas a meeting scheduled at 10:30 a.m. in almost any nonmedical setting meant that you should arrive at 10:25 and be prepared to meet at 10:30 sharp, a doctor's appointment at 10:30 a.m. usually meant a long wait in the doctor's foyer (well-stocked with magazines to peruse, as if 10:30 was expected to come and go without the meeting), followed by another long wait in an (appropriately named) waiting room, and then a meeting with the doctor beginning somewhere near 11:20 a.m. or 12:10 p.m. or even at 12:45.

This was the power of the medical expert in the postwar era. The "Professional Man" walked large in the land. Most people sat and waited rather than getting up and leaving an hour after the supposed appointment time. What real choice did they have? Doctors were the only experts on the topic.

Indeed, this hasn't changed in most places. But a lot of other aspects of health care have shifted since the rise of the Internet.

Yet Another Shift

The increased power of the patient, at least to gather information relating to a diagnosis or course of treatment, is just the beginning of the Information Age revolution in health care. On the one hand, as we already mentioned, a focus on personal wellness and a self-health lifestyle is increasingly popular.

> The increased power of the patient, at least to gather information relating to a diagnosis or course of treatment, is just the beginning of the Information Age revolution in health care.

But medicine itself is experiencing massive change as well. Some of the coming changes may seem a bit like science fiction right now. The suggestion that students would one day be educated mostly by handheld computers and that people would communicate remotely with palm-sized "communicators" or flip phones seemed like a *Star Trek* fantasy in the 1970s.

> A focus on personal wellness and a self-health lifestyle is increasingly popular.

But change happens. Consider some of the major changes to the medical field that are currently in development or early implementation:

- "The Virtual House Call," as an article in *The Atlantic* dubbed a new and growing practice. The article asked: "What if you could text a doctor with a medical question at any time of day and get a quick, thoughtful response? No more haphazard Googling (*swollen feet allergies; tick stuck in ear access to brain?*). No more sifting through random message boards. No more WebMD algorithms suggesting that a vague stomachache might be the first sign of a terminal skin disorder."[96]

Sidebar: The tone of this article is particularly interesting. How quickly people tend to take a new technology for granted and move on to the next. It wasn't very long ago that the idea of Googling your health symptoms or researching them on message boards or sites like WebMD was just fiction. These developments revolutionized health care and were a blessing to a lot of people.

Now many people consider them increasingly outdated. The new thing, at least in this article, is direct personal access to a doctor through technology. So:

- Era 1 (pre-1945): The doctor comes to you.
- Era 2 (1945–2005): You go to the doctor.
- Era 3 (2005–2015): You go online, then (maybe) go to the doctor, and then go online some more.
- Era 4 (2015–?): You go to the doctor/the doctor comes to you by going online, and then afterwards, you go online some more.

Some doctors today worry that such virtual diagnosing and treating will be "disastrous,"[97] much the way many town doctors in the 1940s and 50s warned against the lack of quality they expected from the rise of corporate medicine. (They were right about certain things, it turns out, but not always in the ways they thought.)

However, some medical-field entrepreneurs now say that an online personal doctor service, utilizing the phone and home computers with video, as needed, can keep people connected to basic medical care by licensed physicians for around $99 a month.[98] Such programs are already serving many thousands of families in the United States.[99] With higher fees, presumably, even more is possible.

Such doctors can't meet every medical need, obviously, but they can make recommendations and refer patients to specialists and other face-to-face doctors as needs dictate.

- The concept of "Concierge Care"[100] is also spreading. This occurs where individuals or families pay an upfront monthly fee and then have access to doctors as needed—not online but face to face at the doctor's office. The idea is simple: to pay the doctors instead of insurance companies[101]—and to pay doctors a basic amount each month instead of turning them into bill collectors who have to document each service and then hunt down whoever is going to pay the bill.

As a *TIME* magazine report summarized this model of health care, the goal is to: "Make the patient, rather than the paperwork, the focus of the doctor's day."[102]

This system was developed before Obamacare, and during the Great Recession, it gained popularity.[103] Proponents tout a decrease in paperwork for both doctors and patients and a culture of "no waiting" and "no surprise fees" for patients.[104]

The catch, some people point out, is that such doctors are able to serve far fewer patients than typical primary care physicians.[105] But supporters of Concierge Care say this is a benefit, not a problem. It creates more personal focus and a relationship between doctors and patients and is a step toward a return of the old-style family doctor.

Another development is to "Seize Control of Your Checkup," as a *Men's Health* report suggests. This article then goes on to teach readers how to do the basic annual checkup tests on your own. Want to check your blood pressure? No problem. Heart rate? Same.

Although you shouldn't downplay the importance of these checkups, the article tells us, with a little effort, you can do your own and do them well.[106] Check your ABSI (body mass index), look over your skin for possible small cancers, and check the inside of your mouth for any bumps, spots, swelling, or bleeding.[107]

Since only one in five men go to a physician annually for a checkup,[108] and "72 percent of doctors say their fellow docs order unnecessary tests,"[109] you could be ahead of the curve by doing your own checkups—not just annually, but even more often.

The idea is that in the era of wellness, we should take initiative and not rely solely on health-care professionals to keep an eye on our health.

- Alternative doctor visits are also increasingly popular. These include retail clinics, where you just walk in without an appointment and ask the physician, dentist, ophthalmologist, or other doctor any question that arises concerning your health. Such clinics are now available in many stores like Walmart, Target pharmacies, CVS, and Walgreens.[110] Nurses and physician's assistants sometimes staff these clinics; other times, doctors are there as well.[111]

> **The idea is that in the era of wellness, we should take initiative and not rely solely on health-care professionals to keep an eye on our health.**

Another such alternative model is found in e-visits with your normal family doctor, which allow you to skip the foyer and the waiting room.[112] A growing number of doctors allow such appointments. As one report put it: "Take one tablet and Skype your doctor in the morning."[113]

A third kind of alternative doctor visit is the "group visit" or SMA (shared medical appointment), where you schedule a checkup or seek the doctor's help on a given concern with your whole family or a group of friends. This saves time and costs for everyone involved.[114]

- The concept of tracking technology is also being widely discussed. This means that a wristband—with or without an interactive watch face—or some other instrument could be worn on our bodies and track our health.[115] This mobile technology would allow wearers to keep track of their blood sugar, heart rate, miles walked each day, calories expended, the air quality over the course of the day, the calories in what they eat, and much more.

  Or less. Individuals could program the tracker to monitor the factors they care about and leave other functions dormant. For example: How much pollen is in the air today? (If you have allergies, this could be very helpful.) How many calories are in those cheese fries? (You can check the calories before you order. "That many calories, huh? Wow! I'll take the chicken salad.") What's the traffic like on the freeway versus the back roads? What's my body temperature?

  Such devices could be developed in smart watches, connected with the Internet, and upgraded with memory—to house your medical records, for example, and compare current bodily conditions with your health history. Theoretically, such devices could warn you on a fall morning:

> *The conditions today are similar to those that preceded you getting a nasty cold the last two Septembers. It's recommended that you take extra vitamin C and wear a light jacket, even if you don't think you need it.*

Or simply:

> *It's likely to rain today. Take your umbrella.*

This technology is in many ways similar to some advanced smartphones or in-car personal electronic assistants, but with more intimate features designed to support your health. The device could also link directly to your doctor. In fact, much of this is already being done.

Of course, there are numerous important privacy concerns attached to such technologies. But whether or not you personally use such devices, in the new untethered era of technology that people like Steve Jobs and Elon Musk have pioneered, a world where a lot of people believe a child should "receive his or her first smartphone" at age one,[116] mobile personal health trackers (or whatever they end up being called) will likely be popular.

- Implanted tags are also a real possibility. This is a more controversial variant of the mobile health tracker technology mentioned above, and it is often referred to in reports or publications simply as the "RFID (radio frequency identification) tag."

The Atlantic reported on this in interesting terms: "RFID tags are now so small that they could fit in a watch, or even under your skin. (Such implants aren't science fiction: one techie, Amal Graafstra, has written about how he installed RFID tags in his hands and RFID readers on various doors in lieu of locks, so that he wouldn't have to bother with keys anymore.)"[117]

Such tags could be designed to gather health information, like the readings listed above in the discussion of mobile health trackers. The health benefits could be intriguing. The legal and governmental ramifications of such developments will likely be a lot more controversial.

Wellness

Indeed, in the emerging era of self-health and wellness, it is increasingly important for every citizen to be informed about breakthroughs, technologies, ethical challenges, and the legal/moral issues associ-

> In the emerging era of self-health and wellness, it is increasingly important for every citizen to be informed.

ated with health care. Eating well and getting appropriate exercise are a great start, but real wellness encompasses a great deal more.

If our society is to increase its health in the economic, social, moral, and political realms, today everyone needs to be actively involved—keeping an eye on developments in all aspects of life and taking an effective stand for family, freedom, and goodness.

Health care isn't just about health anymore. Wellness is the emerging new focus. Beyond this, or as a part of it, we need to know what brings wellness—to our bodies and to individuals and also nations—and focus on this.

A misplaced emphasis on "sick care" has dominated our society for too long. The problem is that when our experts and institutions focus on dealing with sickness, they tend to forget about wellness.

Again, this is true in the health field, and it is true in technology, business, education, and politics as well. And these fields are increasingly intermeshed. A refocus on wellness and self-health in our society thus necessitates a holistic approach: we need to take a good hard look at health, not only physical health but also the health of our family, educational, career, economic, moral, and political worlds.

> It is up to us as individual citizens and leaders to do something.

All are lacking wellness in significant ways. It is up to us as individual citizens and leaders to do something about it. This is the message of this chapter on wellness, and it is also the message of all seven paradigm shifts covered in this book.

We must put wellness—physical, spiritual, educational, moral, economic, and political—at the center of our lives. This is a call for leaders in the twenty-first century. They are desperately needed.

PARADIGM
7

Community Is the New Neighborhood

It is not from the benevolence of the butcher, the brewer, or the baker that we expect our dinner, but from their regard to their own interest. We address ourselves, not to their humanity but to their self-love.

—ADAM SMITH

Geography was destiny.

—STEVEN PINKER

Communities exist because their members benefit from the associations. If such benefits turn to burdens, people generally leave. This explains the current shift in modern communities.

If you grew up in a "1950s-style suburban community," you experienced a bit of utopia. In fact, such communities

> Communities exist because their members benefit from the associations.

existed long after the 1950s, often in small towns or exceptional neighborhoods. In the words of Christopher Lasch:

> We wanted our children to grow up in a kind of extended family....A house full of people; a crowded table ranging across the generations; four-hand music at the piano; nonstop conversation and cooking; baseball games and swimming in the afternoon; long walks after dinner; a poker game or Diplomacy or charades in the evening, all these activities mixing adults and children — that was our idea of a well-ordered education.[118]

Add to this food on long tables with homemade tablecloths, cans of drinks shoved into barrels of ice, and celebrations at the local park; races for every age on every holiday and parades with more participants from the neighborhood families than spectators watching; families who walk door to door in the evenings, stopping to speak with elderly couples on every porch; a loud siren that can wake up the whole town at any time of night or interrupt school, church, or any other event at any moment of the day and send members of the volunteer fire department racing away; muddy swimming holes and a national wardrobe of cutoff jeans; watermelon offered — in triangular shapes of all sizes — by adults on the street to passing youth as freely as air. This was a culture widespread.

Such idyllic communities became part of the American psyche, built on the shared personal experiences of many or through the media with Mayberry (*The Andy Griffith*

Show), Mayfield (*Leave It to Beaver*), Bryant Park (*My Three Sons*), or the idealized neighborhood of Milwaukee where *Happy Days* took place.

These shows were extremely popular for a generation and created a national sense of what the 1950s-to-1970s era was like for many families. Indeed, the name "*Happy Days*" sums up the majority view of the period. While it is certainly mythical to suppose that this was the norm everywhere, as argued by Marc J. Dunkelman in *The Vanishing Neighbor* and by others, it was unquestionably a fair portrayal of many such neighborhoods.

Culture Defined

But what if you grew up in a very different kind of environment? You would have faced different challenges, learned different lessons, and likely even adopted different values. As Steven Pinker put it:

> Culture, then, is a pool of technological and social innovations that people accumulate to help them live their lives, not a collection of arbitrary roles and symbols that happen to befall them.
>
> This idea helps explain what makes cultures different and similar. When a splinter group leaves the tribe and is cut off by an ocean, a mountain range, or a demilitarized zone, an innovation on one side of the barrier has no way of diffusing on the other side.[119]

In similar fashion, when children leave home and make their way in the adult world, they respond to various challenges that are different from those they faced as children and different from those their parents faced. They innovate, marry, and have children, and the culture of their new home is different in some ways than the home they grew up in.

> When children leave home and make their way in the adult world, they respond to various challenges that are different from those they faced as children and different from those their parents faced.

The values may not change, but the way of expressing those values in relation to new and different experiences alters culture. The culture a spouse brings to the home also influences and alters the whole arrangement—in small ways if nothing else.

As the iconic Thomas Sowell has wrote: "A culture is not a symbolic pattern....Its place is... in the practical activities of daily life, where it evolves under the stress of competing goals and other competing cultures."[120] And a community is a culture in itself, one made up of a group of people who voluntarily interact because they benefit from the mutual associations.

> A community is a culture in itself, one made up of a group of people who voluntarily interact because they benefit from the mutual associations.

Even More Important

But there is another facet to community, brought on by the central role of adults to pass on wisdom, knowledge, skills, and important ideas to the young. The reason for this may be self-interest, but often a genuine interest for the next generation, and for the community itself, is even stronger.

Indeed, in real community, Mortimer Adler argues, "More than interest is needed. Teaching, Augustine declares, is the greatest act of charity. Learning is facilitated by love."[121]

Community, like the association of parents and children in a family, is a two-way street. Love is often a bigger motivation than any kind of material self-interest. Aristotle taught that community is simply an outgrowth of family, a larger kind of family.

In fact, what makes a group into a true community is that leaders feel that the success of those they serve is just as important as their own personal success. The interests of others are as important to leaders as their own interests—to the point that leaders "own" all the interests of the community.

Without this care of leaders for others, and the honor of others for the leaders, no genuine community exists. Such bonds often occur within a family. When they form beyond family, when authentic, heartfelt community is established because leaders feel a keen supportive (not controlling) interest in the success of those they serve, this is something special.

Origins of Community

Community of the type we've been considering seldom happens in the modern world. It was the norm in tribal society, however. After all, the tribe was created by children growing up, getting married, and then raising children of their own. With five or six married couples and their children, plus grandparents—the parents of each of the married adults—you have a tribe. And the parental bonds create that feeling in the leaders that "the others' interests are *my* interests." Family naturally does this, and it organically spreads in a tribal system.

This dominated the Nomadic Age. But with the advent of the Agrarian Age, it all changed. In short, the Agrarian Age brought with it the pyramid structure of society we discussed earlier. In the new arrangement, the general's interests were usually quite different from those of the foot soldier, the peasant's interests were different from those of the manor lord, and the king's interests were different from the interests of the courtier.

The top-down pyramid model dominated the Industrial Age as well. If anything, it became stronger. Those at the top benefited very little from the interests of individuals in the middle or at the bottom of the stack. Factory owners needed workers, yes. They depended on them, in fact. But they didn't need any certain individual. They could typically fire you (or your father) and fill the vacant spot before the afternoon shift.

Likewise, as the Industrial Age progressed over time, many a CEO could issue pink slips to a whole department, watch stock values rise, and replace the entire department in some low-tax international destination—and build a new building to boot—at a substantial savings to the firm. Oh, and the savings in employee benefit costs under the new nation's laws…what a windfall for shareholders!

Cheers would erupt at the next board meeting. The interests of management were certainly not the interests of the "Organization Man" employee. There were exceptions to this cold reality, but again, they were rare.

Bring It Forward

Compare the education of the young in the tribe to the norm in Agrarian and Industrial Age classrooms. In tribal societies, how well each youth could hunt and fight meant the difference between prosperity and ruin for the tribe, clearly in the direct interest of the teachers and mentors. In the classroom, however, if a student failed, the interests of the teacher weren't directly hurt, at least as long as some of the students excelled.

Hence the one-on-one mentoring, the close and heartfelt coaching, and the hours and months and years of personalized attention by a seasoned adult for each young learner in a tribal culture. Such measures were deemed too costly in

> In a tribal culture, education for each young learner centers on mentoring; close, heartfelt coaching; and hours, months, and years of personalized attention by a seasoned adult.

Agrarian and Industrial Age schools, which focused as much as possible on efficiency rather than effectiveness, depth, and painstaking quality.

No, in the pyramid model of schooling, the assembly line, it was enough to get the basics to most of the students and a quite decent education to a few "A" students. The interests of the leaders were seldom the same as the interests of the rest. If you have ever had a teacher who made your interests his or her guide, however, you know the amazing things that can come from it.

The suburban communities of the 1950s and the cul-de-sac neighborhoods of the 1980s sometimes made this leap.

After all, if you are a parent in such an environment, your children's interests are your interests, and with such proximity and closeness to other families, their influences on your children's culture and upbringing naturally become your interests as well. This is where community arises and thrives, as mentioned.

Community often happened in churches during the Agrarian Age, and it sometimes happened in church groups during the factory blue-collar and later "Organization Man" white-collar periods of the Industrial Age. As Robert Putnam showed in his study of modern communities and their decline, community sometimes happened in what can only be called "sports communities," such as the parents and town boosters of a local little league or high school team or the urban bowling leagues of the 1960s.

Community even coalesced around a few professional sports teams over the years.

In fact, Putnam's title is instructive: *Bowling Alone: The Collapse and Revival of American Community*. His words express the modern longing for "community lost," frequently sounding a bit like an epic Milton poem. Putnam wrote:

> We tell pollsters that we wish we lived in a more civil, more trustworthy, more...caring community....
>
> Americans are right that the bonds of our communities have withered, and we are right to fear that this transformation has very real costs.... Creating (or re-creating) [it] is no simple task. It would be eased by a palpable national crisis, like war or depression or natural disaster, but for better and for worse, America...faces no such galvanizing crisis. The ebbing of community over the last several decades has been silent and deceptive.[122]

Still, his recommendations for reviving community show little innovation. He hopes we will "spend less time traveling and more time connecting with our neighbors" and that we'll get to know more of our neighbors by their first names.[123] He outlines a number of similar ideas, including that we hold more "picnics," but most of them center on the old-style neighborhoods, and none of them truly connect with the new models of non-geographical communities. He does hope that at least we'll use the Internet to connect, not just to surf alone.[124]

The Business Challenge

But while many facets of modern life continue to struggle for community, this has been especially true in business — at least since the days of tribal closeness. The commercial system of industrial society rearranged other organizations to support the needs of the corporations. Schools became places to train workers for the various jobs, specialties, and roles of the firm, and families changed their schedules to meet those of the company.

Moreover, instead of families spending most of the day together — as in the tribes and even agrarian communities — industrialism sent the adults off to work and the kids off to school. In fact, the adults and kids were even further separated once they arrived at school or work: Mom and Dad in different departments on different floors (or even in different companies) and children segregated by grade levels.

Days were now spent with people not in your family and not even from your neighborhood in many cases. Evening activities frequently followed the same pattern. All of this was a mirror image of the people in a corporate setting, arranged by roles and functions rather than by natural relationships, likes, interests, or affinity. The corporation ran the era. Even government employees followed the corporate arrangement.

As a result, most neighborhoods naturally lost their intimate sense of community. They became places to visit, in a sense. Adults and youth slept there and ate dinner there (part of the time) but didn't usually spend their entire day there. Fast food made it easier to stay away, television made it easier to escape the community even if you were home for the evening, and travel conveniences meant weekends and vacations were more likely to be spent somewhere else as well.

> **The neighborhood culture became less influential than the school, work, and media culture, so adults had less interest in closely leading it.**

The neighborhood culture became less influential than the school, work, and media culture, so adults had less interest in closely leading it. More fences appeared between homes in neighborhoods across the nation.

Changing Definitions

But when the neighborhood sense of community was lost in many places, nothing significant rose to replace it. Indeed, community itself was largely lost for a majority of people. That sense of shared interests, mutual benefits...it stagnated. And with it went most of our societal leadership.

The very definition of "leaders" changed in these circumstances. Leaders were no longer people who cared as much about your interests as they did about theirs — because your success was their surest path to achieving their own interests. Now "leaders" became pyramid masters, managers from afar who set the rules, measured your performance, and awarded or withheld benefits.

Such "leadership" wasn't the bottom-up striving of successful people to help you truly achieve, all because they loved you because they served you with all their heart and their greatest interests were most benefited when your greatest interests were met. Instead, now "leadership" was all about meeting leaders' interests.

As for your interests, good luck. You were on your own.

Indeed, business even had a new name for this momentous change: the Management Revolution. It would have been sad to call this a leadership revolution, and fortunately they got it right—but just in the naming. It was all about management. In this new model, the manager "managed" the interests of the organization, and the "Organization Man" worked for the interests of the corporation.

The modern corporate organization was even recognized as a "legal person" by the law. Another victory for the corporations and their government partnership. One more level of bricks on the Establishment pyramid. "It's shaping up nicely, Pharaoh," someone must have announced in a New York boardroom or Washington mixer.

"So what exactly is a pyramid scheme?" any modern student of the postwar era has to ask.

Answer: "Have you been to Washington? Wall Street? Madison Avenue? An ivy-covered university? A Big Five bank?"

But where is community to be found? That's the question of our era. Of any human era, really. Imagine Hamlet, chin in his hand, lamenting: "Where is community? That is the question."

The answer is no longer geographical, in most cases. But genuine communities do exist. Again, consider the definition. A true community is a relationship where people feel and treat each other's interests with as much care and love as their own.

A Community Primer

Ask yourself the following questions:

1. Whose interests would you put above your own?
   These are your family.
2. Whose interests would you work for at the same level as your own?
   These are your community.
3. Whose interests naturally benefit your interests, and vice versa (when you achieve, they achieve; when they achieve, you achieve)?
   These are your long-term community.

Human beings flourish most in community. We want community. We seek it. Many leading neural scientists argue that our brains (the physiology of the dendrites, synapses, corpus callosum, and the frontal lobe, for example) seem specifically designed to thrive in community.

> **Human beings flourish most in community. We want community. We seek it.**

The Bible has a long list of calls for community. It is the driving force right out of Eden as well as the ideal to be strived for through the stories of

Abraham, Moses, David, and the early Christian cloisters around the Mediterranean. Just consider the way community was described in Exodus 24:3 (KJV): "And Moses came and told the people all the words of the Lord, and all the judgments: and *all the people answered with one voice...*"[125]

What a community should and shouldn't be was loudly preached by Samuel, Isaiah, and Jeremiah and later expounded upon at length by Paul.

The same issues were addressed in secular history: by Homer in both the *Iliad* and the *Odyssey*, by Socrates and Plato and Aristotle, in Virgil's *Aeneid*, and by Augustine, Aquinas, Luther, Calvin, Shakespeare, and many others.

> **The quest for real community has been, in many ways, the quest of humankind.**

The quest for real community has been, in many ways, the quest of humankind.

Jane Austen apparently dedicated her entire work to the questions surrounding community. What makes true community? What threatens it? What causes it to decline or falter? How can we build it and build it well? How do courtship, marriage, family, and extended family relationships relate to the success or detriment of community?

Any insightful reader of Austen is ultimately faced with the direct, very personal question "What kind of community member are you?" and the corollary "How can you do better?"

But the answer is still fleeting for most people. After all this commentary, all the pages addressed to this incredibly important topic, community remains elusive for many.

The Reason

This is understandable, actually, because the answer is not as simple as most people apparently wish it were. Community is a complex, not a basic. It is more of a paragraph than a simple letter like C or Q. It is, in fact, a bit of an algorithm, not merely a number like 7 or even 144.

But with all that said, it isn't terribly difficult either. It's not rocket science. It is made up of two powerful ideas. Understand them both, and you'll understand community.

We've already mentioned both of these ideas, but it's worth repeating them here and showing how they fit together. The first major idea in community is *benefit*. Community occurs where benefits are shared, where the success of one individual automatically increases the success of the others, and where the achievements of the others benefit the one.

> **Community occurs where benefits are shared, where the success of one individual automatically increases the success of the others, and where the achievements of the others benefit the one.**

This makes sense to most people. It's straightforward. It appeals to common sense. When the baker and the butcher both do well, each benefits from the success of the other. If the baker fails, the butcher's situation is often worsened, and vice versa.

This is the first facet of community: *shared benefit*.

The second factor necessary for community is *genuine love* — authentic caring for the other person(s).

This is likely the reason many people in history have struggled to understand community, much less find and build it. What, exactly, do we mean? Simply that in human history, the ideas of direct, personal benefit and self-interest on the one hand and loving care for others on the other are usually considered opposites. Enemies. In competition with each other.

This is usually taught as a zero-sum game, meaning that if love increases, self-interest must decrease. Or if self-interest expands, love must shrink. This is the message spread by dozens of popular human philosophers, from Cain and Nimrod in the Bible to Machiavelli and Caesar, Hobbes and Marx, Lenin and Mao, and many others.

In the classic novel *Moby Dick*, one ship captain's obsession with his chosen enemy, a great white whale, creates this same narrative: a choice between love and benefit. No other option is given, suggesting that in fact there are no other possibilities.

This is frequently taught as the plight of the superhero, from Batman to Superman to the Green Arrow: be strong and benefit the community, or give in to self-serving love and be unable to remain strong. Self-interest is always wrong in such stories. The same is true of the great myths, from Hercules or Thor to Athena and Dionysus.

Humans have long convinced themselves, and their young, that we must choose between love on the one hand and self-interest on the other.

But where does that leave community? If, as we have stated, community is the fusion of these two characteristics — love and self-interest — then most of our traditional mythologies and heroic stories teach that community is impossible.

Again, it's not surprising that genuine community is rare under such circumstances. If a leader, teacher, book, or movie emphasizes the importance of love, critics naturally respond with how the message forgot about self-interest. If instead the leader or book focuses on the importance of self-interest, a chorus of critics shout the message down as greedy, self-centered, selfish, and even angry and mean.

The Core of Community

Make no mistake: community flourishes where we find a way past the two extremes and blend the necessary ingredients: genuine love and genuine self interest. This is incredibly motivating for both individuals and groups.

> Community flourishes where we find a way past the two extremes and blend the necessary ingredients: genuine love and genuine self-interest.

And this is the genius of authentic community. It fuses the shared tendency to desire a safe place, surrounded by friends who have your back no matter what, with the individualistic cry for self-expression, freedom to reach for your own greatness, and power to let loose your inner Rascal.

This Is So Deep!

Community is incredibly powerful precisely because it gives freedom, encouragement, and voice to both of these great needs and desires. It simultaneously offers the warmth of home, hearth, and smiling hugs along with the pedestal, sweat, cheers, and trumpets of personal victory. It is the standing ovation and the motherly hug all at once.

> A community caught in the extreme of either comfortable hearth alone or battle and triumphant pedestal only isn't really community.

A community providing anything less isn't worthy of the name. A community caught in the extreme of one or the other (comfortable hearth alone or battle and triumphant pedestal only) isn't really community.

The Capstone

But how does all this work? How is it possible to bring together two such diverse streams of human emotion and endeavor? The answer is organic, as basic as male and female joining to bring about shared goals that are much greater than what is possible to either gender on its own.

The key word in this is *service.*

This process is deeper than first meets the eye. Here is how it works. It can start in one of two different places. First, it can start with love. When we truly love, we serve. If we don't serve, as Shakespeare assured everyone, we don't actually love.

When we love and serve, an interesting thing happens: our interests begin to mesh with the interests of those we love and serve. They become parallel interests, at least. If we continue to serve, they become common interests, and with enough service, they become truly shared interests.

Eventually, our interests are the same as those of the ones we love and serve. Again: If they achieve, we achieve. If we achieve, they achieve. When this happens, we are part of a community.

There is a second way this can occur. It begins with self-interest. We serve someone for the same reason the baker serves the butcher—because he or she benefits from the arrangement. It is clearly self-interested.

But with enough service, something begins to change. It turns out that not only do we serve those we love, but we also naturally begin to love those we genuinely serve.

The more we serve, the more we begin to care. The more our interests and those of the person we are serving become parallel, then, with enough time or effort, they become common. And eventually service, even in the name of self-interest, develops into shared interests.

Where we don't voluntarily serve, this magic doesn't happen—in either of these two ways. But where service is real and either long-lasting or very demanding, or both, it transforms into both love and shared interests.

It Works

While this may seem overly philosophical in this format of reading words from a book, it is a discernible and living phenomenon when experienced in real life. If you truly serve, you do it out of either love or some kind of self-interest—and when you give great service, you naturally develop love and shared interests.

This is the power of community. It is a relationship, built on both practical and emotional bonds. And such relationships, forged between people and God or people and other people, are among the strongest connections in the world. Community is a powerful thing.

Marriages built on love, mutual benefits, and genuine, consistent service are incredibly powerful. So are family relationships and community bonds built on these same three factors.

Other Examples of Community

Where church relationships reach the same level—authentically mutual benefits, deep and long-term service, and love—religious community thrives. The same with education. In the military, they call this becoming a true "band of brothers."

A few such communities are found online in the modern world. Although there is a lot of negativity on the Internet, and far too many threads, discussions, forums, posts, tweets, and other communications seem committed to griping, gossiping, or fault-finding, some connections get past this and build positive, quality community.

When you find such communities that resonate with your values and goals, it is often very enjoyable and very helpful to take part. Again, your service to others will determine how much you truly become part of, and benefit from, your associations.

> **Your service to others will determine how much you truly become part of, and benefit from, your associations.**

And once in a while, rare but wonderful, a neighborhood can still achieve community. If you experience this, up your service and help it thrive. It will be more than worth it.

The New Reality

With all this, in the post 9/11 era, it is in business that such communities are most prevalent. This is still rare, even in business, but it is growing.

Imagine business connections with a community focus. Such a model would have to be structured so that the success of leaders is directly the success of workers, and the success of workers is directly the success of leaders. If some achieve, their leaders achieve. If some fail, their leaders feel that failure directly and immediately. And vice versa.

It would also need to be designed in such a way that service to those you lead is what brings concrete financial as well as other types of success. This can create a business where service is the entire agenda, and such authentic levels of service will naturally turn self-interest into shared interests and love. That kind of service will also turn love into shared interests and increased service.

Such a model—in education, church, military, online, or in business—will turn the modern pyramid structure of society on its head. This transforms leadership from distant lecturing and what often amounts to symbolic posturing to close, personal friendship, love, mentoring, brotherhood/sisterhood, and leaders up late nights working their guts out in the same room or on the phone *with* you to meet *your* needs—because they genuinely, deeply care about you and your dreams and goals.

Community rocks! Along with family, it is the best system humanity has to offer. It is the best way to really get important things done. It is the best way to live.

It is, in fact, a formula for happiness and progress.

> **Community rocks! Along with family, it is the best system humanity has to offer.**

In the post-1945 era, a number of great neighborhoods achieved this powerful level of bonding. Today, in the post–Great Recession world, such communities—now available mostly in the powerful relationships found in truly great business groups—*are* the new neighborhood.

CONCLUSION

Why Trend #4
(Building a Business Is the New Career)
Is the Most Important

And the Lord said unto Gideon, By the three hundred men that lapped will I save you, and deliver the Midianites into thine hand: and let all the other people go every man unto his place.

—JUDGES 7:7 (KJV)

Predicting the future is like baseball: If you hit 300 out of 1000, you're doing really well. If you're hitting 400, you're the best of the best.

—ANONYMOUS

The future is difficult to predict, for the simple reason that it hasn't happened yet. You don't know what you don't know, and the future is still ahead.

It is better to *forecast* then, rather than try to predict.

But what's the difference? Many people use these words interchangeably. Aren't they pretty much the same thing?

Two Different Methods

The answer is no. They are very different. According to the *Oxford English Dictionary*, the word *predict* means to "state that an event will happen in the future."[126]

From the same source, *forecast* means to "estimate a future event or trend…especially of the weather or a financial trend."[127]

Prediction attempts to tell what *will* happen and to do so in detail and with some level of precision. Forecasting, in contrast, emphasizes what might happen. It is an estimate of what is likely, of what is probable or even possible. Not what *will* come, but what reasonably *could* come.

In the Bible, the two are treated very differently. Consider the following:

> Boast not thyself of to morrow; for thou knowest not what a day may bring forth. (Proverbs 27:1, KJV)
>
> Whereas ye know not what shall be on the morrow. (James 4:14, KJV)

Then compare:

> Now learn a parable of the fig tree; When her branch is yet tender, and putteth forth leaves, ye know that summer is near.… And what I say unto you I say unto all, Watch. (Mark 13:28, 37, KJV)

It doesn't make much sense to take heed, watch, and pray, unless heedful watching will somehow help.

Take ye heed, watch and pray: for ye know not when the time is. (Mark 13:33, KJV)

It doesn't make much sense to take heed, watch, and pray, unless heedful watching will somehow help. And the example given is that while you can't perfectly predict the specific moment when summer will come, you'll learn a lot about what's happening by noticing that the leaves are starting to appear on the trees.

Becoming Watchmen

The commandment to watch, or be watchful, is given many times in both the Old and New Testaments, and indeed the idea of leaders as "watchmen" runs through the Old Testament. Watchmen watch and warn, not because they know every detail but because they can see the patterns, cycles, trends, and other signs and evidences of things that are likely ahead.

> **Watching and forecasting are part of leadership.**

Watching and forecasting are part of leadership. And top leaders know that watching the horizon ahead is a key role in providing quality leadership to the members of their communities and teams. Leaders estimate the importance of any trend and tell others about the big ones.

Again to the *Oxford English Dictionary*: to *estimate* means to

> **Leaders estimate the importance of any trend and tell others about the big ones.**

form and share "a judgment or opinion,"[128] and something *estimable* is that which is "worthy of great respect."[129]

Part of leadership is having the wisdom to watch what is happening in the world, the judgment to know what is important, and the heart to share such essential information with those you lead.

This is precisely the case with the seven paradigm shifts we've outlined in this book. Each is important. Each is potentially world-changing.

Leaders, and those who want to become leaders, will keep a close eye on all seven. If details change, they'll take note and rearrange their thinking according to the new information. If major events cause further additions to these seven, they'll put them on their list and share them with those they lead, love, and serve.

Most important, leaders help those they lead learn to think about trends, patterns, and cycles and become watchmen in their own right. Reading history and great books and ideas is vital to developing this ability to watch and see what is really going on in the current world.

A review of the seven paradigm shifts we've forecasted in this book shows that each has the potential to drastically change the world we live in:

Networking Is the New Media
Families Are the New Education
Mentors Are the New College
Building a Business Is the New Career
Principles Are the New Political Parties

Wellness Is the New Health Care
Community Is the New Neighborhood

The Twenty-Year Challenge

These seven changes will impact the lives of everyone, in major, even drastic ways. People who don't know about these seven important shifts, or don't understand them, won't be able to proactively prepare for them.

Indeed, now is the time to prepare. Now is the time to consider these powerful trends and take action in our families, education, business, and other parts of our lives.

As Chris Brady wisely put it: "Twenty years from now, what will you wish you had done today?"

> Now is the time to consider these powerful trends and take action in our families, education, business, and other parts of our lives.

Those who carefully and effectively answer this question, especially in light of the seven paradigm shifts that are remodeling our society in their wake, will be the leaders of the twenty-first century.

The Catalyst

Of all the trends, paradigm shift number 4 (Building a Business Is the New Career) stands out. It is perhaps the most powerful shift sweeping our generation. In many ways, it is driving the other six paradigm shifts—or the culmination of some of them.

Not everyone sees this yet for what it is, and not everyone is taking action to turn it to their benefit. Some, in fact, are holding on to the past, hoping against hope that the emerging reality isn't real.

But many other people are taking this wave of change seriously, and they are making the choices necessary to become leaders.

Orrin Woodward taught that watching the waves is an important way to understand what is happening in the world, but it can't take the place of knowing that the tide is coming in as well. The waves are significant, surely, but the tide is a game changer.

These seven paradigm shifts are the tides of our century, and paradigm shift 4 is the tide of our generation. Indeed, it is shift 4 that will build the leaders who help us thrive in the twenty-first century. Without such leaders, no such flourishing future will occur.

Love or hate these seven paradigm shifts, as you choose. But however you feel about them, they are real, and they are coming. In some cases, as with shift 5 (Principles Are the New Political Parties), we need them to come.

It is up to leaders to take note, take heart, and take action. Each of these seven shifts is an opportunity for increased success, happiness, achievement, and progress. Together they present a generational call to greatness.

> **It is up to leaders to take note, take heart, and take action.**

What We Need

Leaders are needed to ensure that these shifts remain opportunities instead of becoming problems. Leaders are needed to look around and see how these shifts can best help our communities, nations, and world. Leaders are needed to communicate a positive vision of how to use these shifts to better our lives.

Leaders are needed to act, to work, and to build teams that turn the rising trends and tides into great benefits. Leaders are needed now.

The tide is coming.

Who will lead it?

Will You Stand?

We invite *you* to step forward, rise to this challenge, and accept this call — to be like Gideon and his three hundred, who, though small in numbers, acted like leaders.

We must never forget that great leadership changes everything.

If you accept this challenge to lead, it will mean building yourself, building excellent teams, building genuine communities, finding your greatness through service, and in turn serving and loving and helping others find their greatness.

In short, the call of these seven paradigm shifts is the call to leadership.

To you.

Now.

Here.

If you accept it, you will change your life. You will bless the lives of many others. You will put yourself and your family on the path to true community. But this can only happen if you lead.

Our challenge to you is to take a deep breath, make your choice, and dedicate your life to doing just that.

Lead!

NOTES

1   Stephen Covey, *The 7 Habits of Highly Effective People* (1989, Simon & Schuster, paperback), 30–31.

2   Ibid., 29.

3   "The 100-Year March of Technology in 1 Graph," by Derek Thompson, *The Atlantic*, April 7, 2012.

4   See, for example: John Naisbitt, *Mind Set!*; John Naisbitt, *Megatrends* ("Chapter 8: From Hierarchies to Networking").

5   John Naisbitt, *Megatrends* (1982, Warner Books, hardback), 189.

6   Ibid., 191–204.

7   See Jack Lynch, "Every Man Able to Read," Literacy in Early America, *CW Journal*, Winter 2011.

8   Ibid.

9   Ibid.

10   National Center for Education Statistics, IES, State and County Estimates of Low Literacy.

11   See TJEd.org.

12   Alvin Toffler, *The Third Wave* (1980, Morrow, hardback), 29.

13   Ibid., 47–48.

14   Ibid., 385.

15   See Oliver DeMille and Shanon Brooks, *A Thomas Jefferson Education for Teens*.

16   See Chris Brady, *Rascal.*

17   Nassim Nicholas Taleb, *Antifragile,* 255 (advance proof).

18   Ibid.

19   Amazon review, "The Organization Man," June 2015.

20   Wikipedia, *"The Organization Man,"* June 2015.

21   Ibid.

22   Amazon, June 12, 2015, review of the 2002 University of Pennsylvania Press reprint of *The Organization Man* by William Whyte.

23   Brad Plumer, "Only Twenty-Seven Percent of College Grads Have a Job Related to Their Major," *The Washington Post,* May 2013; U.S. Bureau of the Census, 2010 American Community Survey.

24   Amanda Ripley, "The Upwardly Mobile Barista," *The Atlantic,* May 2015, 60–72. See also the "How to Graduate from Starbucks" blog post on amandaripley.com.

25   Thiel Fellowship website, "About the Fellowship," June 2015.

26   Amazon review, "The Higher Education Bubble," May 2015.

27   Kevin Carey, *The End of College* (2015, Riverhead, hardback), 154.

28   Amazon review, "Excellent Sheep," June 2015.

29   Ibid.

30   Ibid.

31   Amazon Review, "College Disrupted," June 2015.

32   See William J. Bennett, *Is College Worth It?* (2013, Nelson, hardback), 205–215.

33   See Thomas J. Stanley, William D. Danko, *The Millionaire Next Door* (1996, Longstreet, hardback).

34   Ibid.

35   See Thomas J. Stanley, William D. Danko, *The Millionaire Next Door*. See also, Robert Kiyosaki, *Rich Dad's Cashflow Quadrant* (2011, Plata, paperback); Andrew McAfee, "Stop Requiring College Degrees," *Harvard Business Review Blog Network*.

36   See Nassim Nicholas Taleb, *Antifragile* (advance proof).

37   Ibid.

38   Ibid., 34.

39   Ibid., 16.

40   Ibid., 171.

41   See Ken Kurson, "Blood in the Water," *Esquire*, September 2010.

42   Chris Brady, *Rascal: Making a Difference by Becoming an Original Character* (2010, Obstaclés Press, paperback), 24–25.

43   Alvin Toffler, *The Third Wave*, 261.

44   Ibid., 261–262.

45   Ibid., 262.

46   Ibid.

47   The original quotation reads: "We set up a system whereby the managers only made money when their salespeople made money. We overlapped the needs and the goals of the managers with the needs and goals of the salespeople." Stephen R. Covey, *The 7 Habits of Highly Effective People* (1989, Simon & Schuster, paperback), 231.

48   The original word was *faction*, which was commonly used to denote political parties in historical writings.

49   David Hume, *Essays Moral, Political, and Literary*, Eugene F. Miller, ed., 56–57. Cited in Oliver DeMille, *The U.S. Constitution and the 196 Indispensible Principles of Freedom*.

50   Ibid., 55–56. Cited in Oliver DeMille, *The U.S. Constitution and the 196 Indispensible Principles of Freedom.*

51   Albert Ellery Bergh, ed., *The Writings of Thomas Jefferson,* 3:339, cited in W. Cleon Skousen, *The Five Thousand Year Leap,* 27.

52   See Oliver DeMille, *The U.S. Constitution and the 196 Indispensible Principles of Freedom,* 199–233.

53   Stephen R. Covey, *The 7 Habits of Highly Effective People* (1989, Simon & Schuster, paperback), 18–23.

54   Ibid.

55   Ibid., 18–19.

56   Ibid., 217–220.

57   See David Brooks, *BOBOS in Paradise.*

58   Ibid., 84.

59   Ibid., 85–89.

60   Ibid., 89–90.

61   Ibid., 90–92.

62   Ibid., 93–102.

63   Ibid., 108.

64   Ibid., 115.

65   Ibid., 216.

66   Ibid., 217.

67   See the A&E version of *Pride and Prejudice.*

68   William D. Cohan, "Can Bankers Behave?" *The Atlantic,* May 2015, 75–80.

69   Quoted in Jerry Useem, "Why It Pays to Be a Jerk," *The Atlantic,* June 2015, 49–58.

70   Ibid.

71   Ibid.

72   John Naisbitt, *Megatrends*, 159.

73   Ibid., 159–188.

74   Ibid., 188.

75   Ibid., 183.

76   Ibid., 131–157.

77   Shell Global Scenarios 2025.

78   Ibid.

79   Ibid., 8–9.

80   "The Real Effects of Binge-Watching TV," *Details*, March 2015, 146.

81   Patricia J. Sulak, M.D., *Should I Fire My Doctor?*, 16.

82   "The Real Effects of Binge-Watching TV," 146.

83   Ibid.

84   Ibid.

85   Ibid.

86   Ibid.

87   Patricia J. Sulak, M.D., *Should I Fire My Doctor?*, 9.

88   Ibid., 63–68.

89   Ibid., 85–94.

90   Ibid., 79–84.

91   Ibid., 95–107.

92   Ibid., 109–126.

93   Ibid., 127–123.

94   Meghan O'Rourke, "Doctors Tell All: And It's Far Worse Than You Think," *The Atlantic*, November 2014, 112.

95   Summarized by Meghan O'Rourke in "Doctors Tell All: And It's Far Worse Than You Think," 110–122.

96   James Hamblin, "The Virtual House Call," *The Atlantic*, November 2014, 38.

97   Ibid.

98   Ibid.

99   Ibid.

100   David Von Drehle, "Medicine Gets Personal," *TIME*, December 29, 2014–January 5, 2015, 49.

101   Ibid.

102   Ibid.

103   Ibid., 50.

104   Ibid., 51.

105   Ibid., 52–54.

106   Paige Fowler, "Seize Control of Your Checkup," *Men's Health*, January/February 2015, 75–78.

107   Ibid.

108   Ibid., 76.

109   Ibid.

110   Ibid.

111   Ibid.

112   Ibid.

113   Ibid.

114   Ibid.

115   Yves Behar, "Bring the Doctor with You," *TIME*, March 24, 2014, 46.

116   See, for example, "The Technology Issue," *The Atlantic*, November 2014, 83–-84.

117   "Scan Me Now," *The Atlantic*, April 2015, 28.

118   Quoted in Susan Pinker, *The Village Effect*, 267.

119   Steven Pinker, *The Blank Slate* (2002, Viking, paperback), 65.

120   Quoted in ibid., 67.

121   Mortimer Adler, "Education," *The Great Ideas: A Syntopicon*, 2:381.

122   Robert Putnam, *Bowling Alone*, 402–403.

123   Ibid., 408.

124   Ibid., 410.

125   Emphasis added.

126   *Compact Oxford English Dictionary*.

127   Ibid.

128   Ibid.

129   Ibid.

Subscriptions and Products from
Life Leadership

Rascal Radio Subscription
Rascal Radio by Life Leadership is the world's first online personal development radio hot spot. Rascal Radio is centered on Life Leadership's 8 Fs: Faith, Family, Finances, Fitness, Following, Freedom, Friends, and Fun. Subscribers have unlimited access to **hundreds and hundreds** of audio recordings that they can stream endlessly from both the **Life Leadership website** and the **Life Leadership Smartphone App.** Listen to one of the preset stations or customize your own based on speaker or subject. Of course, you can easily skip tracks or "like" as many as you want. And if you are listening from the website, you can purchase any one of these incredible audios.

Let Rascal Radio provide you with **life-changing information to help you live the life you've always wanted!**

The Life Leadership Series
(also available in Spanish and French)
The Life Leadership Series subscription is specifically designed to foster personal growth and development across all areas of life. Consisting of four audios and a specially chosen book each month, this material will help develop new and lasting habits that can have a massive impact over time.

Series includes 4 audios and 1 book monthly.

Audios available in physical and digital versions. Receive a physical book regardless of format selected.

The AGO (All Grace Outreach) Series

We are all here together to love one another and take care of each other. But sometimes in this hectic world, we lose our way and forget our true purpose. When you subscribe to the AGO Series, you'll gain the valuable support and guidance that every Christian searches for. Nurture your soul, strengthen your faith, and find answers to better understand God's plan for your life, marriage, and children.

Series includes 1 audio and 1 book monthly.

The Edge Series

You'll cut in front of the rest of the crowd when you get the *Edge*. Designed for those on the younger side of life, this hard-core, no-frills series promotes self-confidence, drive, and motivation. Get advice, timely information, and true stories of success from interesting talks and fascinating people. Block out the noise around you and learn the principles of self-improvement at an early age. It's a gift that will keep on giving from parent to child. Subscribe today and get a competitive *Edge* on tomorrow.

Series includes 1 audio monthly.

The Freedom Series Subscription (12 Months)

Freedom must be fought for if it is to be preserved. Every nation and generation needs people who are

willing to take a stand for it. Are you one of those brave leaders who'll answer the call? Gain an even greater understanding of the significance and power of freedom, get better informed on issues that affect yours, and find out how you can prevent its decline. This series covers freedom matters that are important to *you*. Make your freedom and liberty a priority and subscribe today.

Subscription includes 1 audio monthly for 12 months.

LLR Corporate Education Program

Based on the *New York Times* bestseller *Launching a Leadership Revolution*, the LLR Corporate Education Program is designed not just to *train* your employees but to gradually and effectively *develop* your existing talent into engaged, contributing, go-to leaders and systemically create a permanent culture of leadership that affects every employee within your organization.

For a small investment, you can make a dramatic difference in your workplace environment. Fill your company with high-performance leaders who are proud to leave their "signature" on their work. Every month, a new session (each containing 1 leadership book and 4 audios) is conveniently shipped directly to your office or to each participant's home.

Courses include 1 book and 4 audios monthly. Optional tests included at no additional charge.

LLR Corporate Education Program Course 1 (6 Sessions)
This is where Life Leadership's corporate revolution began. Firmly establish a leadership culture throughout your entire workforce with the 6 monthly sessions of LLRC Course 1.

LLR Corporate Education Program Course 2 (6 Sessions)
Keep up the leadership momentum LLRC Course 1 started, and build on it with LLRC Course 2 to further increase employee engagement, productivity, and retention.

LLR Corporate Education Program Course 3 (6 Sessions)
LLRC Course 3 shifts gears a little bit and begins applying the concepts learned in Courses 1 and 2 by considering an interesting and very broad array of case studies.

LLR Corporate Education 12-Month Program Courses 1 and 2 (12 Sessions)
Establish and solidify a leadership culture throughout your workforce over the period of a year with the LLRC 12-Month Education Program, which includes all of the materials from LLRC Courses 1 and 2. Definitely a longer term option for the savvy employer.

LLR Corporate Education 18-Month Program Courses 1, 2, and 3 (18 Sessions)
The momentum will stay in full effect with the LLRC 18-Month Education Program, which includes all of the materials for LLRC Courses 1, 2, and 3. Experience lasting results and effectiveness that allow for ongoing success and help to attract high-caliber new talent to your organization.

FINANCIAL FITNESS PROGRAM

Get Out of Debt and Stay Out of Debt!

FREE PERSONAL WEBSITE

SIGN UP AND TAKE ADVANTAGE OF THESE FREE FEATURES:

- Personal website
- Take your custom assessment test
- Build your own profile
- Share milestones and successes with partners and friends
- Post videos and photos
- Receive daily info "nuggets"

FINANCIAL FITNESS BASIC PROGRAM

The first program to teach all three aspects of personal finance: defense, offense, and playing field. Learn the simple, easy-to-apply principles that can help you shore up your resources, get out of debt, and build stability for a more secure future. It's all here, including a comprehensive book, companion workbook, and 8 audios that amplify the teachings from the books.

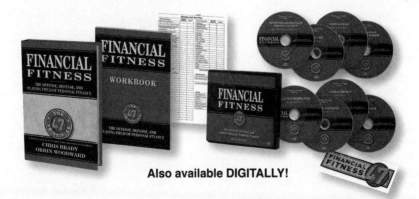

Also available DIGITALLY!

FINANCIAL FITNESS MASTER CLASS

Buy it once and use it forever! Designed to provide a continual follow-up to the principles learned in the Basic Program, this ongoing educational support offers over 6 hours of video and over 14 hours of audio instruction that walk you through the workbook, step by step. Perfect for individual or group study.

6 videos, 15 audios

FINANCIAL FITNESS TRACK AND SAVE

The Financial Fitness Program teaches you how to get out of debt, build additional streams of income, and properly take advantage of tax deductions. Now, with this subscription, we give you the tools to do so. The Tracker offers mobile expense tracking tools and budgeting software, while the Saver offers you thousands of coupons and discounts to help you save money every day.

The Life on Life Initiative

SETTING PEOPLE FREE

At Life Leadership, we are committed to setting people FREE. We realize that everyone is different, that people start at different places, and that some don't get much of a chance to start at all. The Life on Life Initiative helps to bridge that gap.

What

The Life on Life Initiative is a Life Leadership–sponsored program dedicated to helping people gain FUNCTIONAL FREEDOM through literacy and other necessary life skills. It involves three levels of contribution from both corporate employees and Life Members: 1) financial contribution, 2) awareness campaigns, and 3) "Life on Life" volunteerism where we give of our time directly to those in need.

Why

To whom much is given much is required. We believe our privileges are not merely for our pleasure, but for a larger purpose. Helping those who cannot help themselves is a key part of our overall stewardship.

How

To begin with, for every Life Leadership subscription, $1 is given each month to promote literacy in the markets in which we operate. Additionally, Life Members and employees (who are given two paid hours per week by the company) volunteer their time directly to help others develop necessary life skills.

To get involved or learn more, visit
lifeleadership.com/LifeOnLife/Index.aspx

"Once you learn to read, you will be forever free."
—Frederick Douglass